To Catch A Tuna

By Captain Al Anderson

MT PUBLICATIONS
MYSTIC, CONNECTICUT

Library of Congress Cataloging-in-Publication Data

Anderson, Al, 1938-
     To catch a tuna / by Al Anderson.
          p.   cm.
      ISBN 0-929775-03-1: $9.95
      1. Tuna fishing. I. Title.
SH691.T8A43   1990
799.1'758–dc20

                                     90-21980
                                         CIP

Illustrations by Bob Jones

**MT
PUBLICATIONS**

MT PUBLICATIONS
P. O. Box 293 • Two Denison Avenue
Mystic, CT 06355

Much of my life has been spent on the water in pursuit of various kinds of fish, either for my clients or my own personal enjoyment. Much of the success and happiness that I've enjoyed over the years is a result of the understanding, support and encouragement of my loving wife, Daryl Anne. Few in my position have a marriage partner willing to forego the many social activities during a busy summertime charter season, or make a mid-day VHF radio call should I be in need of an errand, or accompany me during a stormy late night check of the dock lines. And, on top of that, she takes the invitation to catch a striper in the night time inky blackness of a tidal rip or lean back in the harness on a heavy-weight tuna. For these reasons, and many more, this effort is dedicated to her.

Captain Al Anderson.

About This Book

This book comes about as a result of my winter time slide show presentation on "Tuna Behavior". Back in the early 1980s, I put together a show entitled "20 Fathoms to the Canyon" as a means of getting audiences interested in offshore fishing, with the possibility, of course, of booking my charterboat, the *Prowler*. This show, with editing and additions, grew to become a very popular program. Although the material focused on some of the reasons why tuna behave the way they do, the underlying theme was "how to catch 'em." Like any successful fisherman, it pays to know and understand the habits of one's quarry.

That certain tuna species behave differently than others is fact, but why they do it is still up to supposition. Having spent years observing and learning about the various tunas and bonitos, it soon became obvious why so many in the audience had paper and pencil or tape recorder or camcorder. Unlike many of my associates who feared giving any information away, I felt it would assist my business endeavors, which it has done, time and time again.

Many years ago, prior to my fishing the canyons, I knew little of what to expect. Fortunately for me, I read a few articles by a noted tuna expert, and since then I've yet to have a bad trip. Perhaps, like myself back then, armed with a little more information, you, too, can venture offshore for tuna, be it in your outboard powered boat or your Bertram, and enjoy greater success as a result of my experiences.

Contents

Whether the target is a bonito or bluefin, more and more people are heading offshore for the time of their lives.

Initial Thoughts

Deep in the brilliant blue water a longfin albacore makes its final attempt to reach the safety of the darkening depths, but the drag of line and that of the reel has taken its toll. Now, coming toward the transom as the boat idles along, the well-placed gaff scores and this fish is quickly two-handed into the cockpit. The staccato beat of its tail fades away as clean-up chores begin.

Meanwhile, a few miles inshore of this trolling action, one boat in the fleet is off its ball and slowly circling, the angler fast to a sizeable yellowfin tuna. The line begins to point down, straight down at this five year old fish in excess of 200 pounds. Gloved hand now on the leader, and then pulling, the circling motion of the fish toward the transom makes it easy to put the harpoon dart deep into the fish. Moments later the tail rope connects this fish and the stern cleat, with smiles all around.

Perhaps either or both of the foregoing descriptions have been experienced by yourself, or you are anticipating similar events. Action like this is common on the offshore grounds, and very popular among the members of the angling fraternity. Today, more so than ever before, technology has opened the door for many to experience these offshore scenes. Whether fishing from a trailerable outboard powered rig or a high-speed, custom-built, offshore fisherman, today's navigational equipment, meteorological services, infrared satellite photographs, engine reliability, along with micro-chip space age electronics like VHF radios, fishfinders, radar, etc., allow the coastal fisherman to share in the offshore excitement and thrill of catching a member of the tuna or bonito clan.

What continues to amaze me at slide shows is the number of people in the audience that know little or nothing about what goes on in the way of fishing offshore. Frequently I'm asked if I think they could catch a tuna species from their 19-foot outboard powered rig, and become excited when I indicate it wouldn't be too difficult to do. I quickly add that certain electronics should be aboard, the day's weather forecast evaluated, and a quick check of the safety equipment attended to before leaving the dock. And, it helps to know if there are any fish around. On top of that, certain basic tackle and equipment are needed to round out the list of items required aboard. And I'm frequently asked about whether or not the wake from an outboard powered boat will raise tuna and bonito. For sure, and, depending on conditions and size of the rig, one can easily fish four lines or more trolling from a small boat.

But, before I get into the basics of tackle, techniques, equipment, etc., one other very important consideration at this time is the abundance of the offshore tuna and bonito resources. True, it was better decades ago, but from the mid-Atlantic areas to waters south of Cape Cod, sometime during the summer season, with settled weather, fishermen up and down the coast are catching a variety of these gamesters, and having the time of their lives doing it.

It might be longfin albacore one weekend followed by small yellowfin the next with little or no action for several weeks and then the bonito show up

Returning home from a day offshore. Getting into 30 or more fathoms of water is usually more a result of the weather than the size of the boat.

followed by the school bluefin tuna.

In an attempt to improve their score many anglers turn to learning more about the offshore scene by purchasing videos and subscribing to any one of several of the magazines devoted to blue water fishing. It makes a lot of sense to spend a few dollars on a book such as this compared to the potential cost of hundred or even thousands of gallons of fuel, which, in the end, could earn one only a little in acquired knowledge about the fisheries. True, a book or a video can only provide a brief glimpse of the overall picture, but if it starts the wheels turning, so to speak, it can easily be considered a good investment.

Unfortunately, much of the hype about offshore tuna fishing has focused on the money aspect of this kind of fishing. Advertisements by a major boat builder tells of catching enough fish with their product so as to pay for the boat. Another by a monofilament line manufacturer that their product has more strength but less visibility to the fish, prompting more success and profit than lines by other manufacturers. Now, don't misunderstand me; if you've got a high quality valuable fish or two in the boat with a ready fish buyer back at the dock, it makes sense to market these fish. Unfortunately, what has happened as of late is that people go tuna fishing, not for the fun and excitement, but strictly for profit. If the fish don't bite that day, they have a miserable time of it, or, if they are offered 25 cents less a pound than their friend got the previous day, they are outraged. Then there are those who envisioned paying for their new boat with tuna profits. You might even know of someone who mistakenly believed this. Catching any member of the tuna tribe can be loads of fun, and if you manage to land a valuable fish, which can be sold to help defray expenses or increase your arsenal of tackle, fine. But don't let making money get in the way of having a good time. The sale of an occasional fish is simply a bonus.

The offshore scene typically begins in June and can last into November, depending on the weather. Getting into 30 or 40 or more fathoms of water is usually more a result of the weather than the size of the boat. More so than other species, the Atlantic bonito, false albacore and bluefin tuna push in closer to shore than their cousins, at times right in sight of the beach. So there usually comes a time during the season when one does not have to venture too far off. In fact, I've seen boats go speeding off, running right past the fish, particularly in late summer. But more about that later. The point here is that one doesn't necessarily have to go way over the horizon to enjoy catching several tuna and bonito species.

Obviously the offshore waters are a significantly different environment than inshore waters, and one has to recognize and become aware how conditions can affect the fishing, when to employ particular techniques, how to recognize clues to the presence of fish, understand various behavior patterns, use important tools, avoid basic mistakes, etc. It's a whole different ball game than inshore, and it takes a preliminary learning period before one can become comfortable, confident and proficient at catching these ultimate gamesters. But just about the time you expect to get a smashing strike from a bigeye or yellowfin tuna, an oversize white marlin jumps on and, as the line quickly melts off the spool, your confidence disintegrates. That's all part of the challenge of the offshore scene.

Over the years the author has accumulated a compliment of reels for offshore fishing. Some of them were purchased second-hand and have seen 20 years of charter boat service.

Venturing offshore for the day, locating and then getting a bite or two from some sizeable fish, not making any critical mistakes during the battle, and then returning home with high quality fish has got to be the ultimate saltwater fishing challenge, and a certain amount of pride comes from doing it. One of the things that tends to hold some people back from getting involved in the offshore scene is the cost of tackle and equipment. As I indicated earlier, it's not very expensive at all if you keep your common sense. Sure, it's expensive if you rush out and purchase a brand new twin diesel sportfisherman, a half dozen bent butt and straight butt outfits, big game chair, outriggers, etc. Naturally, if you set your sights on giant Atlantic bluefin tuna you're going to need some hefty tackle, 80 pound class at least. But, if you set your sights on smaller bluefin and other species, 50 pound class tackle will more than get the job done. Tackle designed to catch bass and bluefin will be more than adequate on the variety of bonitos that are available. In fact, one should give some consideration to the use of heavy freshwater tackle for these lightweight species. The next chapter focuses on profiling each of the seven different tuna that are commonly available.

Over the years I've managed to accumulate a collection of reels, several of which will soon have nearly 20 years of charter/commercial service. They were chosen because of readily available parts as equipment like this gets its share of abuse when fishing is hot and some clients are somewhat inexperienced. In fact, several of those reels were purchased as used tackle, at a very reasonable price. I think they went to sea but three or four times, perhaps never taking a fish, and went on to be sold when their owner lost interest in the offshore tuna scene. You know, part of the fun of fishing is taking time to evaluate and price various tackle and their levels of sophistication. If you can afford the reels, fine; but most of us cannot. Less expensive models, perhaps with a little less flair, are more than adequate to do the job. Like I said earlier, use a little common sense when it comes to making decisions about tackle.

Back in the dark ages of offshore tuna trolling, you either used a cedar jig or a jap feather. Today the variety of terminal tackle boggles the mind, but more importantly, one can easily afford a basic selection of lures. In the chum slick, cable and single strand wire are no longer preferred. Mono is now in high favor. The biggest expense here comes from the purchase of several flats of high quality bait, be it herring, mackerel or butterfish, for the day. But, viewed as part of the overall picture of expenditures, it's not excessive, and balanced by the savings in fuel when anchored.

I'm sure many will agree with me that freshly caught albacore or yellowfin steaks on the grill rank as some of the finest seafood available. Putting a few steaks in the freezer for a later time will serve to remind you of your success. Perhaps that's reason enough to keep you thinking and planning more trips. Hopefully, some aspect of this book will help you improve your score in the offshore scene.

Fisheries experts list 21 different members of the tuna and bonito families. This book is concerned with six members of the tuna tribe and one from the bonito tribe.

CHAPTER TWO

What Did You Catch?

Most saltwater fishermen would have little trouble identifying a particular fish as either a tuna or bonito, but would be hard-pressed to make an exact identification. The information provided herein will, hopefully, make the identification of a fish you catch somewhat easier should there be any question. A special note of thanks goes to the International Game Fish Association (IGFA) for permission to use drawings and descriptions of the various species.

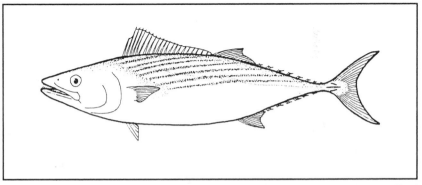

Atlantic Bonito *(Sarda Sarda,* family: *Scombridae);* **also called Green Bonito.**

Distribution: Occurs in tropical and temperate waters of the Atlantic Ocean from Argentina to Nova Scotia and from South Africa to Norway. It is apparently rare in the Caribbean Sea and Gulf of Mexico, but does occur there, and is common in the Mediterranean and Black seas.

Features: The majority of *Sarda* species are endemic to the Pacific, which should simplify the identification of this Atlantic species; nevertheless it is often confused with the skipjack or with other Atlantic scombroid species. This confusion need not exist. The bonitos have stripes on the back, not the belly. Also, the Atlantic bonito is noted for its large mouth, the upper jaw of which normally reaches all the way beyond the rear margin of the eyes. The first dorsal fin is long (20-23 spines) and is only moderately, not highly, elevated anteriorly; it tapers off posteriorly in a graduated, even slope, and stops just in front of the second dorsal fin. The second dorsal fin consists of 13-18 rays, followed by 6-8 finlets. The pectoral fins are short and broad. The tail fin is crescentic. The caudal peduncle is very slender and supports a lateral keel on either side. A bony ridge extending from the vertebrae beneath the keels increases the strength of the tail. This bony ridge is an important taxonomic distinction of the bonitos: the more primitive mackerels do not have a bony ridge under the lateral keels, and the more advanced tunas have a more highly developed plate-like, bony extension under the keels. The bonitos are developmentally intermediate between the mackerels and the tunas in that the bony ridge exists but is incomplete, or segmented, rather than fused together into a plate. As with all scombroid fishes, there are also two smaller keels farther back, above and below the main keel.

The Atlantic bonito has a wavy lateral line. The body is covered with minute scales (large, thick scales on the corselet), and is nearly fusiform, though moderately compressed. There are 16-26 large, conical teeth on either side of the upper jaw and 12-24 on either side of the lower jaw. There are 8-21 (usually 10-18) small conical teeth in a single row on the palatines, and there may be a few small teeth in a patch on the head of the vomer. The *Sarda* species have no teeth on the tongue and no swim bladder. Also, the intestine is straight, rather than folded in the middle as it is in *Orcynopsis, Cybiosarda,* and *Gymnosarda* (also of the bonito tribe). There is a total of 16-23 gill rakers on the first gill arch.

Coloration: The Atlantic bonito has 5-11 straight, oblique bars or stripes that run from just below the lateral line backwards to the dorsal fins. It does not have stripes or spots on the belly. The back is steel blue or blue-green. The lower flanks and belly are silvery.

Behavior patterns: This species spawns in spring and early summer, shedding between 700,000 and 6 million eggs. It is pelagic, schooling, migratory, and feeds on smaller fishes and squid, usually at or near the surface. A strong, fast swimmer, the Atlantic bonito is known to skip or leap on the surface when in pursuit of prey. It is usually found in schools 15 to 20 miles offshore.

Fishing methods: Trolling at or near the surface, casting, jigging, or live bait fishing. Baits include small pelagic schooling fishes and squid as well as cut fish, strip baits, or any of a variety of artificial lures.

General: This species is of some importance in the eastern Atlantic where it is fished for commercially. In the western Atlantic it has little commercial value, except off southern Brazil and Argentina. The flesh, which is dark red, is valued by some and held in low esteem by others.

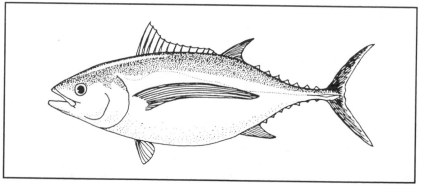

Albacore *(Thummus Alalunga,* family: *Scombridae);* also called Longfin Albacore.

Distribution: Worldwide in tropical and warm-temperate seas, including the Mediterranean: 56°-61°F (13°-16°C). Also found seasonally in colder zones.

Features: The most distinguishing feature of this member of the tuna and mackerel family is its very long, falcate (sickle-shaped) pectoral fins that reach back to a point beyond the anal and second dorsal fins and usually all the way back to the second dorsal finlet. The pectoral fins of certain other adult tunas may also be moderately long, some extending past the origin of the second dorsal fin, but never all the way past the second dorsal fin to the finlets. Moreover, the pectoral fins of these other species would be best described as gradually tapering in shape rather than falcate. Though the very long pectoral fins readily distinguish the adult albacore from other adult tunas, it should be noted that juvenile albacore may have shorter pectoral fins than similar-sized yellowfin tuna *(T. albacares)* or bigeye tuna *(T. obesus).* The albacore can be distinguished from these species at any age by the lack of stripes or spots on its lower flanks and belly and by the presence of a thin, white trailing edge on the margin of the tail fin.

The albacore has an elongate, fusiform body; a relatively short head that does not quite reach to the first dorsal fin; and a broad, crescentic tail fin. The first dorsal fin has 12-14 spines, the second dorsal fin has 13-16 rays, and the anal fin has 13-15 rays. There is very little interspace between the dorsal fins. There are 7-9 dorsal finlets and 7-9 anal finlets. Gill rakers number from 25-32 on the first arch. On either side of the caudal peduncle, there is a strong lateral keel between two small keels. The eyes are large; the liver is striated on the ventral surface; and the body is covered with small scales except for the anterior corselet, which has large, thick scales. The deepest part of the albacore's body is near the second dorsal fin, rather than near the middle of the first dorsal fin as in other tunas, and the vent is round rather than oval or teardrop shaped.

Coloration: The body is dark metallic or steel blue dorsally, changing to silver or yellowish blue on the sides and creamy white underneath. The fins are dark yellowish, except for the white trailing edge of the tail. There is a lateral iridescent blue band. The anal finlets are dark.

Behavior patterns: Pelagic and migratory. Usually remains in deep, clear blue tropical or warm waters, but makes seasonal migrations into colder zones (New England, South Brazil, northern Gulf of Mexico). The young travel in schools close to the surface where they feed extensively on squid and planktonic crustaceans as well as pelagic surface and midwater fishes of all kinds. The adults, which are the object of the longline fisheries, occur deeper and probably not in any large schools. The albacore spawns in the summer, each female shedding between one million and three million eggs.

Fishing methods: Trolling with feathered jigs, spoons and other lures; live and whole bait fishing with mullet, sauries, squid, herring, anchovies, sardines and other small fishes. The albacore is considered by anglers to be an excellent light-tackle game fish.

General: In the United States the albacore is probably the most valuable tuna in terms of quality and profit. Its white meat is canned and sold commercially throughout the country, and is the only kind that can carry the label "white meat tuna."

Commercially it is taken primarily on floating longlines, but also with gill nets, purse seines, and trolled lines.

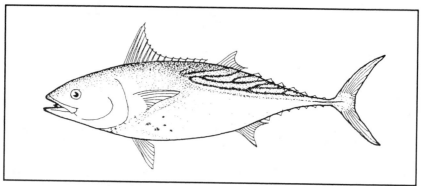

Little Tunny *(Euthynnus Alletteratus,* family: *Scombridae),* also called **False Albacore.**

Distribution: Tropical and warm-temperate waters of the Atlantic Ocean from the New England states and Bermuda to Brazil, and from South Africa to Biscay or Great Britain. Also in the Mediterranean.

Features: The little tunny is most easily distinguished from similar species by its markings (see coloration), but it is also noted for a combination of other features. The first dorsal fin is high anteriorly and very low posteriorly, with a sharply plunging, concave rear margin. The interspace between the first and second dorsal fins is never greater than the diameter of the eye. The second dorsal fin and the anal fin are followed by a number of finlets (about 8 on the back and 7 on the venter). The pectoral and ventral fins are short and broad. The body has no scales, except on the corselet and along the lateral line. On either side of the caudal peduncle, there is a strong lateral keel; and farther back, on the tail, there are two smaller keels. Beneath the main keel the vertebrae of the spine are laterally extended, forming well developed bony supports for the fleshy keels. These extensions and the number and shape of the teeth (20-40 small, conical teeth on each jaw) help to relate the little tunny to the higher tunas, rather than to the bonito or the mackerels. (Bonitos have fewer, but larger, conical teeth, and the bony supports are poorly developed. Mackerels have triangular, laterally compressed teeth, and lack bony supports for the keels.) Unlike its close Pacific relatives, the kawakawa *(Euthynnus affinis)* and the black skipjack *(Euthynnus lineatus)*, the little tunny has no teeth on the vomer.

The little tunny is often confused with the Atlantic bonito *(Sarda sarda)*, the skipjack tuna *(Katsuwonus pelamis)*, and the frigate and bullet mackerels (genus *Auxis*). There are differences among these species, however: the Atlantic bonito has a lower, sloping first dorsal fin; the frigate and bullet mackerels have the dorsal fins set far apart; and the skipjack tuna has broad, straight stripes on the belly and lacks markings on the back.

Coloration: The back is generally dark blue and the lower flanks and belly are silvery white. The little tunny has a scattering of dark spots resembling finger prints between the pectoral and ventral fins that are not

-16-

present on any related Atlantic species. It also has wavy, "worm-like" markings on the back; these markings remain above the lateral line, within a well-marked border, and never extend farther forward than about the middle of the first dorsal fin. If there are any stripes on the belly, they fade quickly after death. The markings are the same as in the closely-related Pacific kawakawa, but are unlike those of any other Atlantic species.

Behavior patterns: The little tunny is a pelagic, schooling, migratory species. Large schools may consist of many thousands of individuals. It is common in inshore waters near the surface, where it feeds on squid, fish larvae, and large numbers of smaller pelagic fishes, especially clupeoids (herring and sardine species). It also feeds on crustaceans. The little tunny comes in closer to shore and is less migratory than the skipjack tuna.

Fishing methods: Trolling or casting from boats using small whole baits, strip baits, or small lures such as spoons, plugs, jigs, and feathers. A few may be caught from shore.

General: Flocks of diving seabirds are often indicative of the presence of a school of little tunny. Because this species feeds on small pelagic fishes near the surface, any school feeding action tends to attract and excite birds looking for a meal.

The dark flesh of the little tunny is esteemed by some and disdained by others. It has some commercial importance.

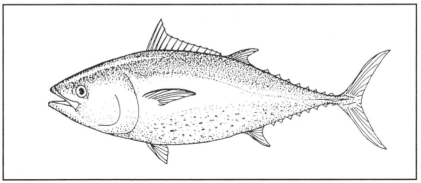

Bluefin Tuna *(Thunnus Thynnus, family: Scombridae).*

Distribution: Occurs in subtropical and temperate waters (56°-84°F, 13°-29°C) of the north Pacific Ocean, the North and South Atlantic Oceans, and in the Mediterranean and Black seas. (Also see behavior patterns.)

Features: The bluefin tuna is the largest of the tunas and one of the largest true bony fish in the sea. It has a stout, semifusiform body that is very slightly compressed, but more nearly round, in cross section. The bluefin can be distinguished from almost all other tunas by its rather short pectoral fins, which measure less than 80 percent of the head length and extend only as far back as the eleventh or twelfth spine in the first dorsal fin. There are 12-14 spines in the first dorsal fin and 13-15 rays in the second, followed by 8-10 finlets. The anal fin has 11-15 rays followed by 7-9 finlets. The bluefin has the highest gill raker count of any species of *Thunnus* (34-43 on the first arch). The bottom of the liver is striated, and the middle lobe is usually the largest. Other features include small, conical teeth; small scales (larger on the corselet); relatively short second dorsal and anal fin lobes; relatively small eyes; a retractable first dorsal fin; a large, crescentic tail; a strong lateral keel on the caudal peduncle; and two smaller keels farther back on the tail.

Coloration: The bluefin tuna is dark blue-black dorsally, paling to silvery white on the lower flanks and belly. The first dorsal fin is bluish, or sometimes yellow, and the second dorsal fin is reddish brown or yellowish. The anal fin and the finlets are dusky yellow edged with black. The lateral keel is black in adults.

Behavior patterns: The bluefin tuna is a pelagic, schooling, highly migratory species. The smallest fish form the largest schools and vice versa. Its migrations, which are among the most extensive in the fish world, appear to be tied to the water temperature, spawning habits, and the seasonal movements of fishes on which the bluefin feeds. Specimens tagged in the Bahamas have been recaptured as far north as Newfoundland and Norway and as far south as Uruguay.

The bluefin's diet consists of pelagic schooling fish (mackerel, flying fish, herring, whiting, mullet, etc.), squid, eels and crustaceans. During spawning, which occurs in the spring or summer, a giant female may shed 25 million or more eggs. Bluefins grow rapidly and may be 2 feet (0.6 m) in length and weigh 9 pounds (4.0 kg) by the end of their first year. By the end of their second year they may be 31 inches (0.8 m) long and weigh 22 pounds (10.0 kg); by age 14 they may be 8-3/4 feet (2.6 m) long and weigh 690 pounds (313.0 kg).

Fishing methods: Trolling with live or dead mackerel, herring, mullet or squid or with artificial lures (spoons, plugs, or feathers); also still fishing with live or dead baits while chumming. Bluefin tuna are supreme in their size, strength, and speed, and are a very important game fish species.

General: The bluefin is an extremely important commercial fish in many parts of the world. The flesh is of good quality, and the annual world catch is significant. The Japanese fishery takes most of the total catch. The bluefin tuna's red flesh is prized in Japan more than that of any other tuna, especially late in the season when the meat contains the most fat. It commands premium prices in Japanese restaurants, where it is served raw.

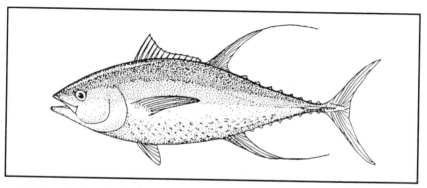

Yellowfin Tuna *(Thunnus Albacares,* **Family:** *Scombridae).*

Distribution: Worldwide in deep, warm-temperate oceanic waters: 60°-80°F (16°-27°C).

Features: Just as the albacore *(Thunnus alalunga)* has characteristically overextended pectoral fins, the yellowfin or Allison tuna has overextended second dorsal and anal fins that may reach more than halfway back to the tail base in some large specimens. In smaller specimens (under about 60 pounds - 27.2 kg), however, and in some very large specimens as well, this may not be an accurate distinguishing factor, since the fins do not appear to be as long in all specimens. The pectoral fins, also, are moderately long in adult yellowfin tuna. They normally measure more than 80 percent of the head length and reach to the origin of the second dorsal fin, but they never reach beyond the second dorsal fin to the finlets as the albacore's do. The bigeye tuna *(T. obesus)* and the blackfin tuna *(T. atlanticus)* may have pectoral fins similar in length to those of the yellowfin. The yellowfin can be distinguished from the blackfin tuna by the black margins on its finlets (blackfin tuna, like albacore, have white margins on the finlets), and can be distinguished from the bigeye tuna by the lack of striations on the bottom of the liver.

The yellowfin tuna has a total of 25-35 gill rakers on the first arch. There is no white, trailing margin on the tail. The body is elongate, semifusiform, and slightly compressed. The first dorsal fin has 12-14 spines. The second dorsal fin has 13-16 rays and is followed by 8-10 finlets. The anal fin has 12-15 rays followed by 7-10 finlets. The tail is large and crescentic. There is a strong keel on either side of the caudal peduncle. The air bladder is present, as it is in all species of *Thunnus* except the longtail tuna *(Thunnus tonggol)*. The body is covered with small scales (larger scales on the corselet).

Coloration: The yellowfin is probably the most colorful of all the tunas. The back is blue-black, fading to silver on the lower flanks and belly. A golden-yellow or iridescent blue stripe (not always prominent) runs from the eye to the tail. All the fins and finlets are golden yellow, though in some very large specimens the elongated dorsal and anal fins may be edged with yellow. The finlets have black edges. The belly frequently shows as many as 20 vertical rows of whitish spots.

Behavior patterns: The yellowfin tuna is both pelagic and seasonally migratory, but it has been known to come fairly close to shore. Tagging results indicate that its migrations are not as extensive as those of the bluefin or albacore. Its diet depends largely on local abundance, and includes flying fish and other small fish as well as squid and crustaceans.

Fishing methods: Trolling with small fish, squid, or other trolling baits, including strip baits and artificial lures. Also chumming and live bait fishing.

General: Growth of the yellowfin tuna is rapid, and it is not unusual for a four-year-old to weigh 140 pounds (63 kg).

Previously, large yellowfins with very long second dorsal and anal fins were called Allison tunas or long-finned yellowfin tunas, and the smaller specimens were called short-finned yellowfin tunas in the mistaken belief that they were a separate species. It is now the general concensus that there is only one species of yellowfin tuna.

The yellowfin is highly esteemed both as a sport fish and as table fare; its flesh is very light compared to that of other tunas, with the exception of the albacore, which has white meat. The yellowfin is an extremely valuable commercial fish, and hundreds of thousands of tons are taken worldwide annually by longliners and purse seiners.

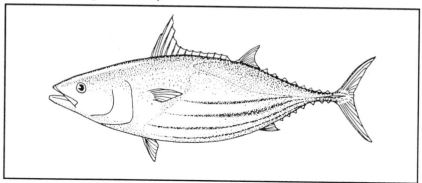

Skipjack Tuna *(Katsuwonus Pelamis,* family: *Scombridae),* **also called Skipjack and Oceanic Bonito.**

Distribution: Cosmopolitan in tropical and subtropical seas, usually in deep coastal and oceanic waters. It is a common species throughout the tropical Atlantic, south to Argentina. It may range as far north as Cape Cod, Massachusetts in the summer months. Occurs most often in temperatures of 64°-82°F (18°-28°C).

Features: The skipjack tuna can be distinguished from most similar species by the stripes on its belly (see coloration). The body is fusiform, elongate, and rounded, and the snout is short and sharply pointed. The first dorsal fin has 14-16 spines and is high anteriorly, plunging into a sharp curve posteriorly, as in the little tunny *(Euthynnus alletteratus).* The interspace between the first and second dorsal fins is never greater than the diameter of the eye. The second dorsal fin and the anal fin are followed by a number of finlets (7 to 9 on the back and 7 or 8 on the venter). The pectoral and ventral fins are short, and the tail fin is broadly crescentic. The body is scaleless except on the corselet and along the lateral line. On each side of the caudal peduncle there is a strong lateral keel; and farther back, on the tail, there are two smaller keels. Beneath the main keel the vertebrae of the spine are laterally extended into a well-developed, plate-like structure, as is typical of the tunas. (These extensions are not as well developed in the bonitos and are absent in the mackerels.) There are about 30 or 40 small conical teeth in each jaw; the teeth are smaller and more numerous than those of the bonitos and are unlike the triangular, compressed teeth of the mackerels. There are 53-63 gill rakers on the first arch, which is more than in any other species of tuna except *Allothunnus* (the slender tuna).

Coloration: The back is dark purplish blue. The lower flanks and belly are silvery with 4 to 6 prominent, dark longitudinal stripes running from just behind the corselet back towards the tail, ending when they come into contact with the lateral line. The presence of stripes on the belly and the absence of markings on the back is sufficient to distinguish the skipjack tuna from all similar species. Though when alive some other species do have stripes on the belly, they have markings on the back as well, and the latter remain the most prominent after death.

Behavior patterns: The skipjack tuna is a pelagic, migratory, deep-water species that may form schools composed of 50,000 or more individuals. In the western Atlantic, skipjack tuna frequently school with blackfin tuna *(Thunnus atlanticus)*, and in the Pacific and Indian Oceans they often school with yellowfin tuna *(Thunnus albacares)*. It is believed that the skipjack tuna may spawn year-round in equatorial waters, and during the summer months in other areas. It feeds near the surface, and its diet consists of clupeoids (herring-like fishes), squids, small scombroids (mackerel-like species), lanternfish, euphausiid shrimps, and crustaceans. The skipjack is a gregarious fish and a fast swimmer.

Fishing methods: Trolling with strip baits, feathers, spoons, plugs, or small whole baits. Some are also taken by casting, jigging, or live bait fishing offshore.

General: The common name Arctic bonito, which is sometimes applied to the skipjack, is a misnomer in both cases. The fish does not range into Arctic waters (see distribution), and it is not a bonito, but a tuna.

In addition to being a highly esteemed light-tackle species, the skipjack tuna has considerable commercial value. It is one of the mainstays of the California tuna fishery and is also of tremendous importance in Japan, Hawaii, Cuba, the Dominican Republic, and other areas of both oceans. It is marketed canned, frozen, smoked, fresh, and dried-salted. In the United States, it is canned with yellowfin and bigeye tuna and sold as light meat tuna.

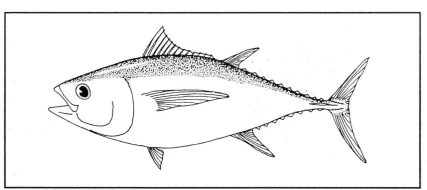

Bigeye tuna (*Thunnus Obesus*, family: *Scombridae*).

Distribution: Found in warm-temperate waters of the Atlantic, Pacific and Indian oceans: 60°-80°F (16°-27°C).

Features: As the name implies, this tuna has characteristically large eyes. The pectoral fins are more than 80 percent of the head length and may reach to the second dorsal fin. The second dorsal fin and anal fins are moderate in size and never reach as far as those of the yellowfin tuna *(Thunnus albacares)*. The bigeye tuna has a total of 23-31 gill rakers on the first arch. The bottom of the liver is striated. The two dorsal fins are close-set, the first having 13-14 spines and the second 14-16 rays followed by 8-

10 dorsal finlets. The anal fin has 11-15 rays followed by 7-10 finlets. The tail fin is large and crescentic, and on either side of the caudal peduncle there is a strong lateral keel between two smaller keels that are located slightly farther back on the tail. The scales are small except on the anterior corselet. The lateral line is indistinct. The body is semifusiform — roundish but slightly compressed. The caudal peduncle is very slender, as it is in all tunas. The vent is oval or teardrop shaped, not round as in the albacore.

Coloration: The back is dark metallic blue, changing through a band of yellow or lighter iridescent blue and becoming a light bluish white color on the lower flanks and belly. The first dorsal fin is deep yellow. The second dorsal fin and the anal fin are blackish brown or yellow, and may be edged with black. The finlets are bright yellow with narrow black edges, and the tail and the pectoral fins may be dark reddish brown or reddish black. The tail does not have a white trailing edge like that of the albacore. Generally, there are no special markings on the body, but some specimens may have vertical rows of whitish spots on the venter.

Behavior patterns: A schooling , pelagic, seasonally migratory species suspected of making rather extensive migrations. Schools of bigeye tuna generally run deep during the day. (Schools of bluefin, yellowfin and some others are known to occasionally swim at the surface, especially in warm water.) The bigeye's diet includes fishes, squid and crustaceans as well as mullet, sardines, small mackerels and some deep-water species. Spawning occurs during the warm summer months. Near the equator it may occur throughout the year. Several million eggs may be shed by each female at each spawning.

Fishing methods: Trolling deep with squid, mullet or other small baits, or with artificial lures; also live bait fishing in deep waters with similar baits.

General: At one time the bigeye tuna was not recognized as a separate species but was believed to be a variation of the yellowfin tuna. The two are very similar in many respects, but the bigeye's second dorsal and anal fins never grow as long as those of the yellowfin, and the two species have different, though variable, colorations. In the bigeye tuna the bottom of the liver is striated and the right lobe is about the same size as the left lobe, whereas in the yellowfin tuna the liver is smooth and the right lobe is clearly longer than either the left or the middle lobe. The number of gill rakers varies slightly too.

As a food fish or as a sport fish, the bigeye tuna is an excellent catch. It is a very important commercial species that is taken predominantly by longlines and sometimes by purse seines. It is marketed canned, frozen, and salt-dried. In Hawaii it is marketed fresh.

CHAPTER THREE

Seasonal Patterns

One of the things the offshore fisherman is fortunate to experience is the wide range of tuna/bonito species that are available to catch, as well as the late spring, summer and early fall seasons in which to do it. What with seven major species available, from June through November, from the DelMarVa to the New England areas, one doesn't have to typically venture too far to find action from these fish. From the giant bluefin tuna to the common (Atlantic) bonito, one runs into major challenges of their angling expertise and skills, whether the fish is taken or not (tagged).

BLUEFIN TUNA

Historically, the large fish (giants) make an appearance on the Continental Shelf south of New England some time in mid-June, typically pushing in from somewhere along the 1,000 fathom edge in their migration from the Gulf of Mexico. If the fish push into the New York Bight area, they then typically turn and move east somewhere along the 30 to 100 fathom edge, pushing on to Cape Cod. Some years they seem to skirt those areas arriving first in numbers in the Gulf of Maine. From late June to late October, these giant fish can be found in U.S. coastal waters, either from New Jersey's famous Mud Hole area, Massachusetts' Stellwagen Bank, or Jeffrey's Ledge. The vagaries of weather, bait supply, season, etc. all work, in most probability, to control the movements and location of these fish which have a reported thermal range of 42°F to 68°F, easily invading the cold, food-rich waters of the Gulf of Maine or Canadian Maritimes.

The medium size bluefin (135-310 pounds) typically show up somewhat after the giants do. Of all the age classes (school, medium, giant), the medium size fish of approximately 200 pounds far outnumber (at this printing) the older, larger fish (over 500 pounds), and will be the predominant quarry for the next few years. They, too, will be available all season long to those fishing from New Jersey to the Canadian Maritimes as long as water temperatures are between 48°F and 66°F.

The school bluefin (14-135 pounds) typically become available in the New York Bight areas and southern New England in late summer. New Jersey anglers are usually the first to see these fish, which, for whatever reasons, pass unseen through the DelMarVa area waters sometime in August. Depending on bait supply, weather, etc., these fish may be in such numbers as to invade southern New England waters by early September. However, the colder waters of the Gulf of Maine rarely see these juvenile fish for the simple reason they have as yet failed to develop thermo-regulatory ability. Decaying fall weather usually brings an end to this near shore fishery as water temperatures fall below 63°F.

BIGEYE TUNA

These fish, typically caught on the edge of the Continental Shelf and seaward (1,000 fathoms), appear not to demonstrate a migration pattern from southern waters as does the bluefin. Instead, it appears they can be

Albacore are worldwide in their distribution. They seasonally migrate into the mid-Atlantic and southern New England areas as early summer waters warm.

found pushing in from the DelMarVa area north along the shelf slope as waters warm in the spring. Conversations with longline fishermen who follow these fish almost on a daily basis indicate that fish in the New York Bight area in June tended to move east (Hydrographers) as summertime waters warmed and then returned west towards Hudson's Canyon as waters cooled around the holiday season. Gulf Stream warm core eddies have a major influence on the movements of these fish along the edge of the shelf with successful rod and reel fishing typically beginning in June and extending into November. (52°F to 66°F preferred thermal range.)

YELLOWFIN TUNA

These fish, common world-wide in tropical and subtropical oceans, are typically found in near surface waters above 18°C (65°F), coming into our waters during the summer months (seasonally migratory). At times, when conditions allow, they have been taken fairly close to shore when near shore waters warm. There is some evidence now to suggest that these fish may concentrate in by those Warm Core Eddies (WCE) that spin off from the Gulf Stream in June and July. Once the WCE reach the Continental Shelf, these fish then disperse as shelf waters warm above 65°F. Typically, the first rod and reel catches occur in mid- to late June, with the fisheries coming to an end as northeasters or northwesters cool shelf waters to below 65°F in the late fall.

ALBACORE

These fish also are world-wide in their distribution, seasonally migrating into the mid-Atlantic and southern New England areas as early summer waters warm. They also show up first along the edge of the shelf, typically in conjunction with the first WCE that encroach onto the shelf, typically in mid- to late June along the mid-Atlantic states and late June or early July off southern New England. It appears that water clarity (blue water) is a strong factor in determining their daily distribution, as is water temperature. Albacore will also push readily into 30 fathoms or less if conditions (clarity, temperature) allow and are probably the tuna species most commonly caught by the offshore troller during the summer season. Like its cousins, it will migrate further offshore as late summer and early fall storms reduce the temperature and clarity of the upper levels of the water column. Although most probably available into early December, the late fall weather produces unpleasant conditions greater than even "diehard" fishermen will tolerate.

SKIPJACK TUNA

These beautifully iridescent members of the tuna tribe are worldwide in their distribution and, in the western North Atlantic, appear on the Continental Shelf north of Cape Hatteras as summer waters warm, by early July off DelMarVa and by early August in southern New England. These gamesters will quickly push into 25 fathoms when conditions allow, striking readily on a variety of small lures used by the troller. A light tackle angler's delight, these fish can offer action well through September during periods of settled conditions. They, too, will depart the near offshore grounds after major fall storms disrupt the clarity and temperature of the upper levels of the water column. Reported thermal ranges for this species are 50°F to 70°F.

FALSE ALBACORE

This gamester, sometimes called "little tunny," is a pelagic, seasonally

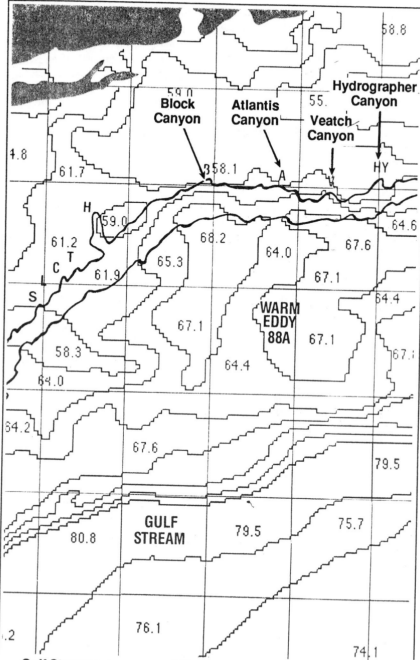

Gulf Stream warm core eddies, like the one shown here south of 40°N, have a major influence on the movements of bigeye tuna along the edge of the Continental Shelf. Temperature chart courtesy of Offshore Services.

migratory species that will hang around on the offshore grounds if it finds things to its liking. Otherwise, it may quickly wind up in late summer just outside the surf line mixing it up with other species, typically bluefish, in its hunt for food. Appearing in numbers typically around or just after the first skipjack tuna appear, they will frequently school together on the offshore grounds. They, too, are a light tackle angler's delight, pulling very hard for their size. It's not uncommon to hear stories from surprised anglers thinking they were connected to a much larger fish. False albacore can be found in waters ranging from approximately 52°F to 70°F, typically starting in July off DelMarVa and August in southern New England. Although chumming on the offshore grounds with very light tackle can be successful, these fish are commonly taken trolling. Should there be only a few fall storms, they may hang around coastal zones well into October or early November where they could continue to frustrate many an angler watching their top water antics under a small cloud of birds.

ATLANTIC BONITO

Typically the smallest member of the tuna tribe seen by anglers, the Atlantic bonito can appear in late June on the offshore grounds north of Cape Hatteras and quickly move to the inshore grounds by early July, having a reported thermal range from 60°F to 80F. However, in the fall these fish may persist along the beach in high bait concentrations well past Halloween in southern New England and well after Thanksgiving in the coastal areas off New Jersey and Delaware. Typically these fish show up en masse on the offshore grounds from DelMarVa to Massachusetts in late July or August and can quickly push in to the 15 to 20 fathom edge where both chumming and trolling can be highly successful. Late summer and fall storms will disperse schools of these gamesters but it is not uncommon to find them biting when pursuing other species, such as stripers or blues.

One of the things the long range canyon fishermen anticipate in the spring is the development of a "staging area" for both yellowfin and longfin albacore. Quite often a Gulf Stream WCE will carry a good body of fish with it to the very edge of the shelf, but the waters of the shelf have yet to warm to the liking of these fish. As a result, very good action can be had on the edge before waters warm to a point where these fish disperse in over it. Frequently, good numbers of fish will then push up into the 40 fathom area before their numbers thin out, typically in late June or early July, offering fast action for those who find them. However, at times the early season yellowfin can be difficult to hook, preferring instead to raise frustration levels as they jump and cavort on and above the sea surface.

Let's take a quick look at the basic scheme of fishing activity as the typical offshore season progresses along with those prey species that are the focal point for particular techniques.

With the exception of the bluefin tuna, those other less glamorous species of tuna/bonito push into and onto the waters of the Continental Shelf each year in pursuit of prey species, typically following a brief period of spawning. In the case of the bluefin, a bee-line is made to the bait/prey rich waters of New England to regain tissue and weight lost over the winter due to the rigors of active spawning. Arriving first on the shelf, these leviathans are hungry, so hungry in fact that they forage on any fish that may be associated with the

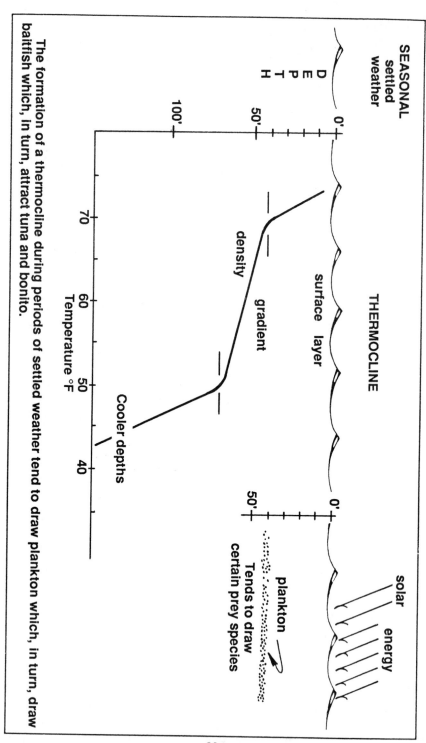

The formation of a thermocline during periods of settled weather tend to draw plankton which, in turn, draw baitfish which, in turn, attract tuna and bonito.

Gulf Weed as it is carried northward by the Gulf Stream. Examining the stomach contents of bluefins caught in mid-June has revealed large numbers of sea horses *(Hippocampus)* along with sargassum itself. The 1,300 mile trek from the Straits of Florida to southern New England offers little in the way of forage. As a result, concentrations of bait, i.e. sand eels, squid, mackerel, can see serious predation by the larger species the moment they arrive.

Typically, by the time the bluefin arrive in southern New England, a WCE has developed in the area of a northern canyon (Hudson, Block, Atlantis, Veatch), with trolling as the technique for getting a strike. For the bluefin, slow-speed trolling with chains and bars of mackerel or squid are preferred, but, at times, a rigged, single-swimming natural bait can do the trick. Offshore in the canyons, high-speed trolling of artificial (plastic) lures brings strikes from the first bigeye, albacore or yellowfin. Trolling usually remains good while water temperatures stay below 68-70°F. On the inshore grounds, trolling is the way to start the season. Once the fish settle down in a given area on local bait, there is a shift over to chumming during daylight hours. In the northern canyons, nighttime chumming typically gets into high gear by late July, but can fade away if waters warm greatly. In the fall, as inshore waters on the shelf cool, action typically resumes in the nighttime on the edge of the shelf as fish return from inshore.

Inshore, several things are going on that can help with the late season fishery, particularly if quantities of bait in the early season were poor. This is the growth and development of squid *(Lolligo)*, butterfish, mackerel, etc. For example, the fry stage of a butterfish in July can be thumbnail size by late August or early September. Squid larvae that were members of the plankton community in June are now several inches in length by early September. As a result, when conditions allow, trolling and jigging on the inshore grounds (inside 50 fathoms) can be red hot as tuna/bonito species work on this growing bait supply.

Along with this transition in the fisheries from trolling to chumming and the seasonal movement of fish onto and off the shelf, there is also a seasonal variation in water temperatures, which many believe is the key to these fisheries. As the vertical thermal structure of the ocean changes, so does the fishing for tuna/bonito species. On the near offshore grounds, where most attempts are made at catching these fish, a phenomenon called thermocline can readily develop under extended periods of settled weather. Typically occuring in the late summer (August-September) when there are days with little or no wind to cause mixing, solar radiation warms the surface layer. Between it and the cooler water of the depths is a strong buffer (density gradient) that prevents mixing of the two. This density gradient works to aggregate members of the plankton community, much like a floor accumulating a layer of dust.

You guessed it! The plankton tend to draw those rapidly-growing juvenile mackerel, juvenile squid, butterfish, etc. which, in turn, attract tuna/bonito species. Areas throughout the thermocline will vary in abundance of plankton and prey/predator species, but will afford both excellent trolling and diamond jigging. Unfortunately, this situation is not a stationary one as currents carry this miniature aquarium along. Loran numbers for hot spots can change considerably from one day to the next. A major storm will produce winds that will mix and churn the upper layers, destroying this phenomenon and the excellent tuna/bonito fishing that can go along with it.

CHAPTER FOUR

Offshore Conditions

The moment the phone rang you knew who it was, and, leaving your tackle job on the workbench, you picked up on the third ring.

"You should have been there. Birds, bait, fish, whales – and we had 'em on constantly for most of the morning. Has to be our best trip ever!"

The first question out of your mouth after hearing this from your friends who's just returned from an offshore tuna venture is "What were the numbers?"

Soon you know the size and kind of fish, what lures worked best, and the general area where all this happened. If all goes well, you anticipate being out there in your boat about 36 hours from now. However, just knowing where to go and what to use are just very small portions of a very large equation. In the few hours that separate your friend's success and your attempts at duplicating it, many, many factors and conditions can change which can drastically affect your chances. Just because your buddy knocked 'em dead Friday doesn't mean you're going to do the same on Sunday.

You probably think that offshore weather is the biggest factor potential in determining your success and, in the opinion of many, that is an accurate conclusion. I continue to be amazed by the number of people who are under the false impression that nice weather is conducive to good tuna fishing. Usually it's the other way around with fish biting the best under dusty conditions. My charter customers, of course, want both excellent fishing and sunny, calm weather. Only rarely does it work that way. In fact, when I indicate that the direction from which the wind is blowing is going to affect their success that day, they look at me as if I've got two heads or just stepped out of a spaceship. But it's a fact – and the sooner you become aware of and accept the fact that conditions will affect your success, the quicker you will become more adept at catching the various tunas and bonitos.

Before I get to a listing and discussion of these conditions, you might want to consider setting up a log book to record success, or lack of it, with a notation of conditional factors. Perhaps, after a while, you'll begin to see a base line of conditions that are necessary for success, which can be used as a guide for future trips. More important is that it will get you to thinking about planning and tackle and equipment to meet those changes that occur, such as having a good selection of leader material aboard to correspond to changing light intensity, depth of the hook bait, water clarity, etc.

The following is a listing of those physical and biological conditions that can affect your success in offshore tuna fishing.

BIOLOGICAL CONDITIONS

1. Fish (kinds, abundance)
2. Bait (kinds, abundance)
3. Birds (kinds, abundance, behavior)
4. Slicks
5. Weeds (kinds, abundance)
6. Marine mammals (whales, porpoises)
7. Jellies (Portuguese man-o-war)

A number of people are under the impression nice weather is best for offshore fishing. Usually it's the other way around; the fish bite best under dusty conditions.

PHYSICAL CONDITIONS

1. Sea water temperature	11. Barometric pressure
2. Sea water clarity	12. Salinity
3. Sea water color	13. Dew point (fog, haze)
4. Thermocline presence	14. Current direction
5. Light intensity	15. Current velocity
6. Dissolved oxygen levels	16. Lunar phase
7. Time of day	17. Tide rips
8. Wind direction	18. Water depth
9. Wind velocity	19. Bottom configuration (contour lines)
10. Sea state	20. Bottom composition

Now that you've looked over a listing of those conditions I feel are significant, let's take a brief look at them.

One of the most important factors controlling the presence or absence of tuna/bonito is the vertical thermal structure of the water column, particularly that of surface and near-surface water temperature. Various species of tuna have thermal preference ranges as do other oceanic pelagic species and you can use this information to improve your success.

Aimlessly trolling around the ocean's surface will only occasionally put a tuna/bonito in the boat. To be consistently successful you need certain valuable tools such as a sea temperature gauge, knowledge of thermal ranges for the various tuna/bonito species, and a copy of the most recent satellite infra-red sea surface temperature charts. Knowing where to go (general area) will save you time and money and, keep in mind, that areas or bubbles of warm offshore water are constantly changing in position, size and temperature. Cold, green water does not harbor most members of the Scombrid family, but warm, blue water with good clarity will, particularly in areas where there are major thermal gradients in sea surface temperatures.

Today, many companies manufacture inexpensive sea surface temperature monitoring devices, but I prefer those offered by Dytek Laboratories, Inc., 165 Keyland Ct., Bohemia, NY 11716; phone 1-800-458-4747 or 516-589-9030; TWX: 510-228-7889.

Probably the most popular source of offshore fishing information is a publication called *The Edge,* produced by Offshore Services, 339 Herbertsville Rd., Bricktown, NJ 08724; phone 201-840-4900. Two basic formats are available, either *The 50 Fathom Report* or *The Canyon Report.* In these reports, one receives highly detailed surface temperature charts, fishing activity reports (loran numbers, lures, etc.), and current information. This service is available from June 15 to October 15, mailed twice weekly, covering the areas offshore of Region 1, Gulf of Maine; Region 2, Long Island and Southern New England; Region 3, New Jersey; Region 4, DelMarVa. Subscription rates will vary depending on the service. The average cost is $168 annually and, if split between several boat owners, is nominal.

Keep in mind that water color and clarity can affect the distribution of these visual predators and are factors which you should attempt to recognize and identify on a routine basis.

With prolonged periods of settled weather, usually in August, inside of 50

Tuna usually feed best under conditions of dim light. That's why those who get to the grounds first thing in the morning usually get some action.

fathoms, large thermocline areas can develop. With plankton attracting bait, predator species such as tuna/bonito can aggregate, with trolling, chumming and diamond jigging producing excellent results. More about that later.

Another factor or condition which can affect your success is what I call light intensity. The concept here is that these fish are visual predators and prefer to do their thing under conditions of dim light. Dim light is an ally for feeding and they demonstrate more aggressive behavior under these conditions. Second, bright light allows them to see better, they become more wary and are apt to shy away when the hook or leader or line is readily visible. Typically, a number of tuna species descend into the darkened depths during daylight hours and is one of the reasons given for poor midday trolling success.

Getting to the grounds with the first light of morning usually results in some action. With low light levels in the upper reaches of the water column, one can experience what we call the morning bite. As indicated, midday can be slow and then, as late afternoon approaches, the afternoon bite begins. Dark, overcast days can extend the morning bite as well as initiate an earlier afternoon bite, again probably as a result of reduced light intensity.

In southern New England, an easterly wind tends to shut off the fishing. For whatever reasons, the fish seem to lose their appetite and don't cooperate nearly as well. Southeast winds tend to blow in warmer water but also brings fog on the inshore grounds. Southwest is our prevailing summertime wind, which I, personally, prefer. Northwest and northeast blow the warmer water and the fish in it further offshore and, if prolonged, can destroy or damage the fishing by altering the nature of the water column, i.e., sea water color, clarity and temperature.

In the trolling mode, flat conditions, particularly on bright days, make it considerably more difficult to get strikes from tuna like yellowfin and albacore. But, let the wind come up with a little white water and, if you can stay over the fish, they become more aggressive and bite better. My guess is the conditions tend to hide or make the terminal tackle less visible, as well as affecting the fish's behavior. As the sea state roughens, in the trolling mode the tunas/bonitos seem to bite better. However, when safety and comfort are compromised, it's time to head home. As conditions worsen, while on the hook and chumming, fish may continue to bite and one can stay reasonably comfortable, but the chances of parting a fish off in the heave increases substantially. After a prolonged period of settled weather, with increasing wind and a falling barometer, there seems to be no better time to be tuna fishing. As more than one fellow has said, "You've got to be careful they don't eat the bottom of the boat away."

In the late summer months, school bluefin tuna and the Atlantic bonito can push in quite close to shore. These green bonito, as we call them, push well into our sounds in pursuit of bait with salinity levels most likely controlling their distribution.

Another condition that frequently stops the offshore tuna/bonito fisherman cold is fog. Safe navigation through busy traffic lanes is facilitated by radar, for sure. This aside, many days visibility offshore is considerably better than inshore for reasons of water temperature. If you're planning on trolling the bars and chains among the whales, it helps if you can see well

Southeast winds tend to blow in warmer water but also bring fog to inshore grounds.

enough to find the whales. For these reasons fog can really put a damper on success.

Trying to visually spot other boats chumming or trolling on hazy days can be risky and, as mentioned earlier, one should plan for such contingencies.

If you arrive on the chumming grounds and find that those anchored up and fishing are suffering with lines going toward the bow because of current direction and velocity, it might pay to drift and chum nearby. Those of us on the grounds daily usually have a means whereby we can adjust the position of the anchor line to the boat, allowing clear fishing of the lines. Again, if conditions change, you've got to make some adjustments. That's the point of this whole chapter.

Let's regress for a minute and go back to wind and sea state. As conditions roughen, you may be forced to troll in the trough of the waves instead of into or down wind. Again, adjust to conditions as they change.

Chumming this particular day, now on the moon, finds the current velocity so strong that techniques that knocked 'em cold just a few days ago no longer work.

At times tide rips offshore act to attract bait and tuna/bonito or act as barriers to their progress and distribution. Usually formed as a result of a strong current set over rapidly changing depths, they can become temporary feeding areas, appearing and then disappearing over the course of several hours either in the a.m. or p.m.

Fish can move very quickly along contour lines feeding, say, along the 25 fathom line. If they are not where they were a couple of days ago, without any major condition changes, they may be further along that contour line. Frequently one sees thermal changes as you cross contour lines seaward, as well as weed lines, bait aggregations,etc. Many long-time tuna/bonito fishermen believe that contour lines act as avenues or corridors for these fish and a few tenths of a microsecond can make all the difference in the world. These same fellows will also tell you that the mud or soft bottom with all its whiting are the reason the bluefin are there. True, the bottom doesn't change, but the season and the forage it may support does.

Let's take a quick look at some of the variables listed under biological conditions. The presence of a number of jellyfish, such as the Portuguese Man-o-war, often indicates a nearby bubble of warm, blue water, usually from a degrading warm core eddy spun off from the Gulf Stream which has now moved onto the Continental Shelf. How far away upwind from your position, the size and magnitude of the thermal edge, kinds and abundance of pelagic species, etc. are secondary to the fact of potential action. If all you've been able to find is cold, green water as a result of prolonged cloud cover preventing satellite imaging, it could be that clue you were looking for.

Typically, those trolling offshore for tuna/bonito encounter two different kinds of seaweed. An abundance of Gulf Weed *(Sargassum)* may indicate the presence of a degrading warm core eddy from the Gulf Stream or the presence of a major thermal edge (sea surface temperature gradient) and, with this, the possible presence of yellowfin tuna or longfin albacore or bigeye tuna. On the other hand, the presence of eel grass *(Zostera)* does not usually indicate increased chances for a smashing strike from an oversized yellowfin. Instead, one typically finds it dangling off the hooks of their lures

An abundance of gulf weed may indicate the presence of a degrading warm core eddy or a major thermal edge.

where it works to prevent strikes from any sensible fish. Many days, not too very far from the beach, trolling for bonito, mounds of eel grass would accumulate in the cockpit as a result of constant tending of the lines. Keeping them clean enough to get multiple strikes was nearly impossible. Under those conditions, one had to work a lot harder to get a strike. This is simply another example of meeting changing conditions.

Most of us, I think, fall into the trap of anticipating the size and kind of tuna/bonito that will be encountered on the offshore grounds on a particular day. A few years back, I recall telling the party about the previous day's fishing for yellowfin tuna with all the excitement we had. With a little luck, they too would soon be hanging onto good numbers of small yellowfin. Approaching the area of the previous day's action, that morning we could see several boats already struggling with fish. Soon we had a smash on the rod fishing out of the starboard rigger. The Green Machine disappeared under a welter of white water, but the whine from the Penn 50W and the bend in the rod indicated no small yellowfin tuna. To make a long story short, three-and-a-half hours later, a 300 pound bluefin tuna that may have thought it was a yellowfin came to the transom. One angler was in the chair for the whole time with no physical help from others in the party. No help, certainly, as two of them, with nothing else to do but watch the battle, decided to put their heads down and sleep. Naturally, by the time we took this fish, the bite was over on the small yellowfin. Believe it or not, I had a disappointed crew on my hands in spite of our success. So much for figuring on the fish.

Then there was the day last season when a friend of mine, fishing in his boat with others, simply knocked 'em cold trolling back and forth under all the birds, watching fish bust into the running bait (mackerel). I was there with a party the next day and – guess what? We never saw so much as a fish, bait, or even a single bird. Conditions had simply changed.

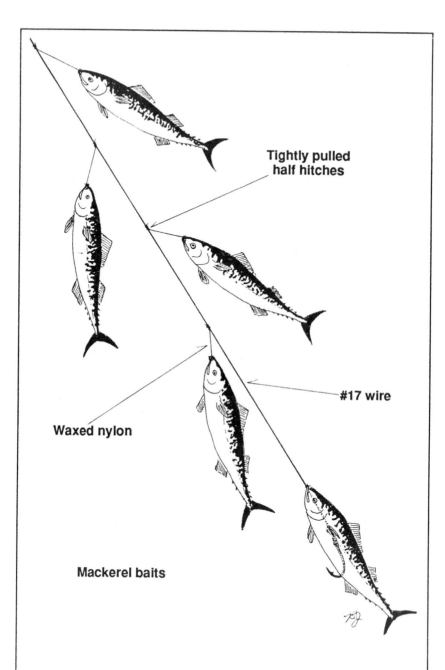

Tightly pulled half hitches

#17 wire

Waxed nylon

Mackerel baits

To rig a daisy chain of mackerel, #17 coffee colored, single strand, stainless steel wire is preferred. Waxed nylon line is used to tie the gills shut and lace each mackerel to a 10 to 12 foot leader. Many anglers favor a nose to tail spacing with the largest bait saved as terminal or hook bait.

CHAPTER FIVE

Slow Speed Trolling

"Which bunch of fish do you want me to steer the boat to?"

"Just keep it going straight while I give the mate a hand getting these rigs overboard and set up the riggers."

Soon all three 80 pound class bent butt rods are in the rod holders flanking the riggers with their respective squid bars trolling as far as 200 feet behind the transom.

"Wow! Did you see that yellowfin over there? It must have been a 150 pound fish at the very least. There's another one! And another one!!"

That late June day in 35 fathoms with little or no wind we saw dozens of yellowfin busting and leaping clear of the surface. Water temperatures at 65° F, trolling slowly now, with one squid bar sporting six-inch urethane squids and the other the nine-inch urethane squids, the *Prowler* was in the midst of a large body of four-year-old tuna. This leaping behavior is thought by fisheries biologists to be a means of thermoregulation in that species.

"We've got an interested party. I just saw a boil on the starboard rig. There he is again!"

Slow speed trolling for giant bluefin tuna originated in the Canadian Maritimes using a daisy chain of mackerel as preferred bait. Today, this technique has evolved to a point in which spreader bars are employed and, although commonly used, those fresh mackerel as well as squid have been replaced by plastic (urethane) imitations. These plastic imitations do work, saving countless hours of time in rigging, not to mention the elimination of all that mess. What's more, this technique has proven effective not only on bluefin but on yellowfin and bigeye as well. In fact, white marlin, blue marlin and mako sharks have been taken this way as well. A common belief is that the fish are excited into biting by the school effect that is created which would not happen if only a single bait was offered. More about that later.

TYPICAL DAISY CHAIN (MACKEREL)

With sights set on giant bluefin tuna, the choice of #17 coffee-colored, single strand, stainless steel wire is preferred. With natural bait, such as mackerel, they are brined to toughen them up, then hand sewn and laced to the wire after the terminal hook bait is rigged. Many prefer to leave the hook (Mustad #77343X) swinging free at the level of the caudal peduncle, others to place all but the point of the hook in the body cavity. A waxed nylon line, for rigging purposes, is used to tie both the gills shut and lace each mackerel to a 10 to 12 foot leader with a series of half hitches. Many favor a nearly nose-to-tail spacing with the largest bait as the terminal or hook bait. Depending on conditions, the number of baits can vary from five to upwards of eleven. When the bellies start to hang out, those baits should be retired as a washed out chain will prompt few, if any, strikes.

TYPICAL SPREADER BAR (PLASTIC SQUID)

With sights again set on bluefin tuna, but this time the smaller fish around

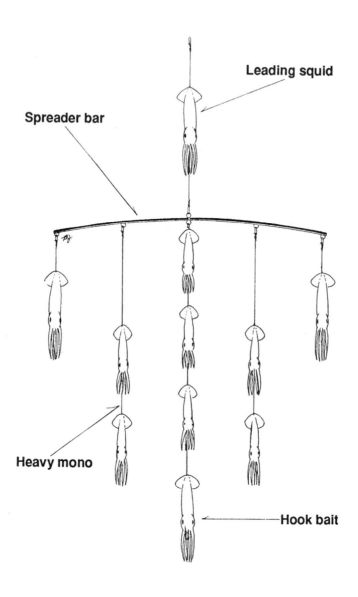

Leading squid

Spreader bar

Heavy mono

Hook bait

A typical spreader bar is usually soft, stainless steel wire with either soldered, crimped or bent eyes for attaching baits. The bar is either lashed with waxed line or crimped to it. Once completed, the rig covers a width of 36 inches and can fish as many as 11 or 12 squids.

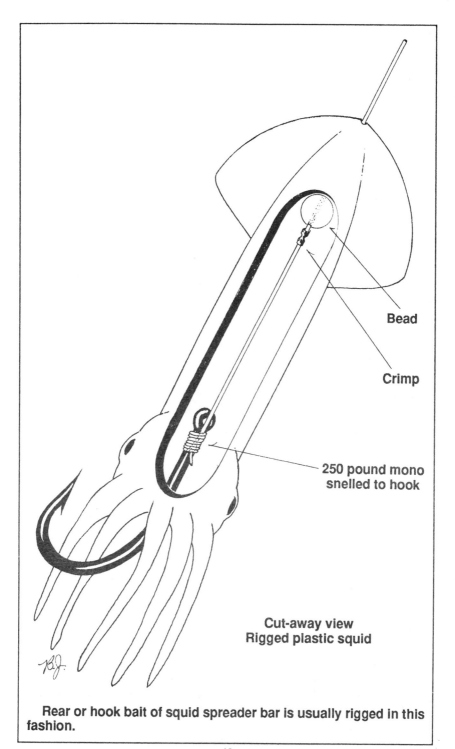

Bead

Crimp

250 pound mono
snelled to hook

Cut-away view
Rigged plastic squid

Rear or hook bait of squid spreader bar is usually rigged in this
fashion.

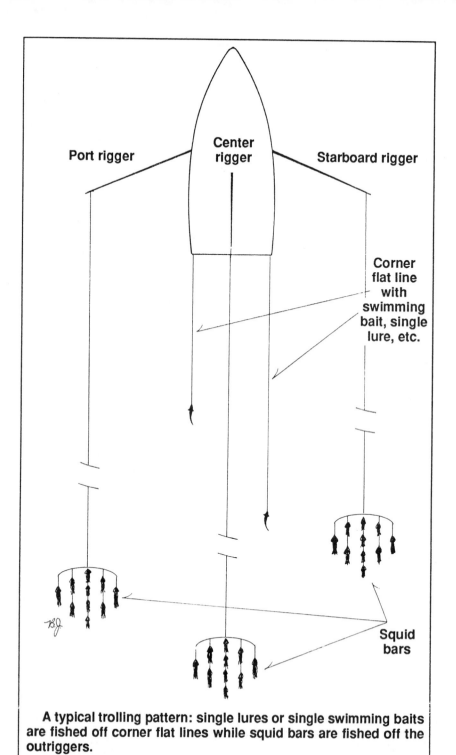

Port rigger

Center rigger

Starboard rigger

Corner flat line with swimming bait, single lure, etc.

Squid bars

A typical trolling pattern: single lures or single swimming baits are fished off corner flat lines while squid bars are fished off the outriggers.

200 pounds, many prefer replacing the single strand wire leader with monofilament in the 200 to 300 pound test range with a ringed eye hook (Mustad #7698B) either crimped or snelled in place. The bar itself, now available from a variety of manufacturers, is typically a soft, stainless steel wire with either soldered, crimped or bent eyes for attaching baits. The bar is either lashed with waxed line to the main leader or crimped to it, spreading to a width of approximately 36 inches and fishing an additional number, usually six, of nine to 12 inch squids. This may bring the total number of squids to 11 or 12. Many prefer to rig their own spreader bars and squids, varying sizes and number of artificial baits which in turn usually determines the size (7/0 to 12/0) of the hook in the trailing bait. Squid colors range from hot pink to natural to lime green with translucent red being favored by many as the best all-around color.

Lately there has been a trend toward slow trolling for early season yellowfin and bluefin with spreader bars that have smaller (six inch) squids in greater numbers, perhaps mixing with larger (nine inch) squids totalling upwards of 24 to 30 squids per bar. These rigs represent a substantial financial investment for anyone and special care is taken to keep them away from marauding bluefish which can destroy a valuable rig in seconds. Many who use these rigs carry a good supply of spare squids, materials and tools to repair and replace those damaged by tuna, bluefish or simply lost during the fight with a sizeable tuna.

Typically, the spreader bar or daisy chain is attached to a straight butt 50, 80 or 130 pound bent butt outfit. Trolling slowly allows considerable time to elapse from the moment of the strike to when the line comes tight. Therefore, quite a few anglers gun it ahead to speed things up. Drags should be set moderately tight as considerable pressure is required to pull the hook out of the bait and into the hard tissue of the fish's mouth once the outrigger clip has released. Many experienced in this mode of fishing set their RUPP Nok-outs or AFTCO Roller-Trollers up as tight as possible to aid in setting the hook when the strike comes.

Small, outboard powered rigs can easily troll the two chains or bars provided they are equipped with outriggers. A third line, down the middle, somewhat closer to the transom, can be done easily. A larger boat sporting a center rigger can readily troll three chains or bars while, at the same time, using one or more lines for either rigged swimming baits or single lure lines. As many as five lines can be fished when the wind and sea conditions allow. The typical trolling pattern for three lines sees the center line fishing the farthest back, with lines for swimming baits and lures closer.

Slow speed trolling the chains and bars (three to four knots) allows the tuna ample time to look things over carefully before deciding to strike. The common rule of thumb is to troll just fast enough to get the baits up and working and then keep them there. For many boats, particularly large, twin diesel craft, in-gear idling speed is simply too fast (five-plus knots) for this kind of fishing and one engine has to be taken out of gear. Fishing natural baits at excessive speed will soon destroy them even if they are toughened up with brine or Formalin beforehand. The plastics, on the other hand, will, if properly rigged, fish easily at a somewhat higher speed.

Along with slow speed, line elevation is critical to success, particularly on

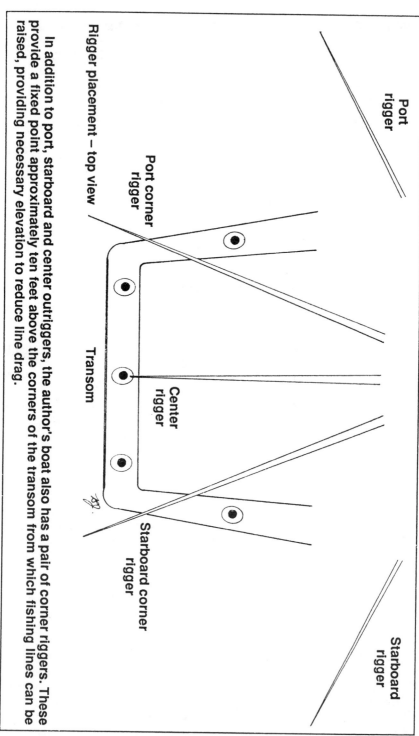

Rigger placement – top view

Port rigger

Port corner rigger

Transom

Center rigger

Starboard corner rigger

Starboard rigger

In addition to port, starboard and center outriggers, the author's boat also has a pair of corner riggers. These provide a fixed point approximately ten feet above the corners of the transom from which fishing lines can be raised, providing necessary elevation to reduce line drag.

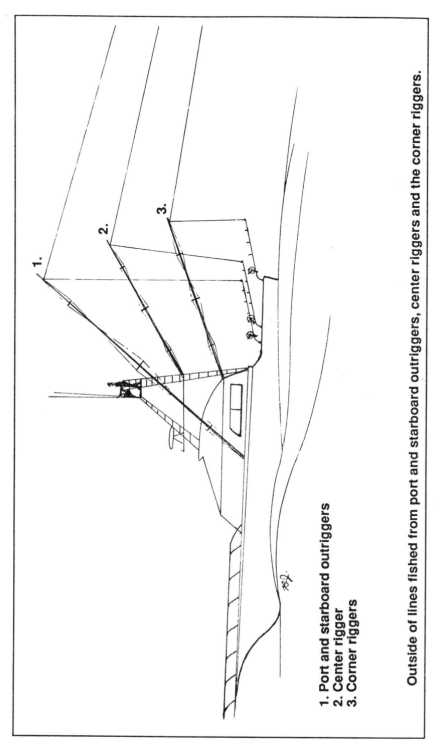

1. Port and starboard outriggers
2. Center rigger
3. Corner riggers

Outside of lines fished from port and starboard outriggers, center riggers and the corner riggers.

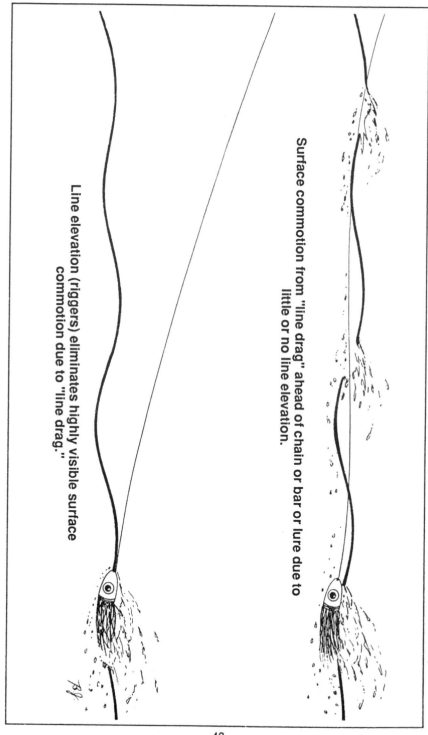

Surface commotion from "line drag" ahead of chain or bar or lure due to little or no line elevation.

Line elevation (riggers) eliminates highly visible surface commotion due to "line drag."

those days when flat conditions prevail. At a slow speed, the surface commotion made by each of the mackerel or squid readily draws the fish's attention, whereas on days when there is a lot of white water the chains or bars appear less conspicuous. On these flat, calm days, the line immediately ahead of the chain or bar can also create considerable surface disturbance. Some anglers go so far as to prevent the swivel at lines end from entering the water for fear that the fish will shy away from this unnatural disturbance. Tuna have keen eyesight and, at best, are very cautious, refusing to strike for the slightest reason.

There have been days when success could be had only by going to a lighter line and leader on the chains and bars. On those days when lines are fishing way back, lines simply cannot be elevated high enough to prevent them from causing some surface commotion.

Years back, I recognized the need, on certain days, to prevent or eliminate highly visible surface commotion resulting from what I call line drag. Setting up a couple of tag lines from the tower flag extensions/supports worked, but were a pain. With bent butt rods in the sternmost rod holders or big game chair arm holders, rod tips had little or no elevation. As a result, the *Prowler* now has a set of what I call corner riggers. These provide a fixed point about ten feet above the corners of the transom from which the fishing line can be raised, providing the necessary line elevation. As with other riggers, lines are set by means of a clip attached to a cord running to the rigger end eye from the base pulley.

Today, any well-stocked tackle shop catering to the offshore fisherman carries a supply of the various artificial squids. The following is a list of current major manufacturers, popular sizes and colors:

M & M Tackle, P. O. Box 2154, Hyannis, MA 02601

Mold Craft, 501 Northeast 28th St., Pompano Beach, FL

Smoker Baits, Custom Mounts International, Inc., Warwick, RI 02887

Ocean Lure Concepts, P. O. Box 323, Chatham, MA 02633

North Pacific, 3731 Moncton St., Steveston, B.C. VTE 3A5

Now that you've invested a near fortune in several artificial squid bars, don't for one moment think you have the key to success in your pocket. The last several seasons, trolling the bars for early season bluefin and yellowfin saw a fair number of fish totally ignore these expensive offerings and zero in on either a single Green Machine, a small chain of hard-head plastics or a rigged, deboned swimming mackerel with a sinker under its chin. Dropped back approximately 100 feet from the transom, fishing directly to the rod tip, these increased the menu selection and brought a surprising number of strikes.

One of the things I take pains to do, and, I'm sure, others do as well, is to see theat the hook orientation in the plastic squids is correct. Because of the somewhat oval body design and lateral anterior fins of these molded baits, they tend to plane along on either of their two flattened surfaces. As the trailing (hook) bait goes over the transom and into the water, I double and triple check that the bend of the hook is in a vertical position. The rationale here is that this reduces the visibility of the hook as seen from below and nearly eliminates fouling with seaweed.

Little in the way of tuna fishing can match the thrill and excitement of slow

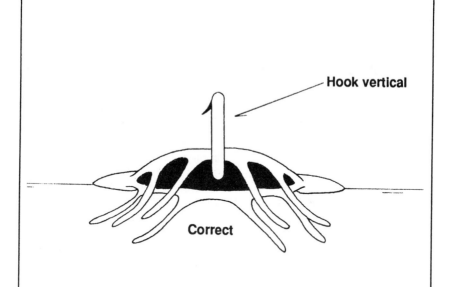

Hook vertical

Correct

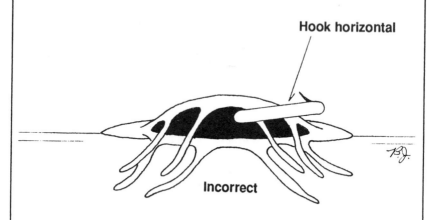

Hook horizontal

Incorrect

Figure 8
Trolled squid – Rear view

trolling a mackerel chain or squid bar in front of a school of subsurface giant tuna. In the tower, quartering the fish in an attempt to intercept them with the baits is difficult at best, not to mention that wind on the water, other boats competing for your position and boats with fish on that have to be avoided make this type of fishing a considerable challenge. Watching the fish swimming along, watching your baits, seeing that boil behind as a half-hearted strike attempt is made and then a gush of white water with the rigger straining backwards until the clip tension is overcome, listening to the reel click as its song increases several octaves, being told that a boat immediately in front of you has just hooked up, with puffs of diesel smoke at the transom from tardy turbochargers to verify the fact, punching the throttle and spinning the boat to avoid having the lines hooked to those jumbo Maguro from cutting one another should they suddenly cross are all part of fishing when the bite is on. There's nothing quite like it when you're hooked up.

Jim Jenrette, owner of the Cape Charles, Virginia, Fishing Center, took this 90 pound tuna while trolling at the 26 Mile Hill. When fish are down 50 feet, the chances of getting them to rise to your wake are poor. However, if the fish are down 15 to 25 feet, the chances of getting strikes are much better. Photo by Gary Diamond.

CHAPTER SIX

High Speed Trolling

It's usually at the end of my slide show that I say a few words about common mistakes made in offshore high speed trolling. One by one, I carefully explain the dos and don'ts and it goes something like this: now that you've finally found the fish and gotten a bite, punch the memory button of the loran. Just like tossing a marker buoy over when drifting for fluke, these fish are living in a particular "spot". Now you have a reference point to which to return on the next high speed troll. Aimlessly trolling over the sea surface leaves success to chance, whereas if you jot down the numbers and then erase the memory, you can quickly return to the spot where you had the bite.

I then usually go on to explain another common mistake I call "Chinese fish" which goes like this: strike – zing – pow! Following the strike, the line zings off the reel and then goes pow as it breaks due to the drag being overly tight. (Zing pow – sounds like a Chinese name, get it?) This usually happens after the outfit has taken a good fish with the drag lever being pushed up or star drag twisted to higher pressure towards the end of the struggle. Then, for whatever reasons, one forgets to ease the drag back to a moderate setting. Drag pressure on reels was made adjustable so that people like you and I could control line pressure better during the struggle.

Another common mistake is the failure to realize that you may have suddenly passed over a large school of fish, be it albacore, yellowfin, etc., and now have one fish on. You then slow the boat down to idle speed or, worse yet, take it out of gear. Gone is the chine wake and propeller turbulence that attracted the fish to your high speed lures in the first place. As a result, you missed the opportunity for multiple bites. Instead, you should have kept the boat going or, better yet, surged it with the throttle, precipitating that second, third or fourth bite or, as I call it, pack attack. By surging the boat you trigger additional fish into striking. With larger fish you may run the risk of dumping a reel, but, then again, you may find but one school of fish all day so this surging maneuver maximizes the potential for strikes, action and fish in the boat.

The list of common mistakes goes on and on but, before ending, I want to say a few words about rushing to take the lines and lures out of the water following a strike from a sizeable fish. For whatever reasons, people feel compelled to remove line and lure from the water quickly, probably to avoid a tangle. Well, I've never caught a fish with a lure that was lying on the deck or gunnel. Leave them in the water because that's where the fish are. So what if one is about to tangle with another? Simply pass that rod, with a smaller fish, either over or under the other to prevent such a tangle. Idling along with lures subsurface, members of the same school have obliged more frequently than you might imagine. And, having to pull all lines in and then get all lines out again, especially upwards of nine rods, is not all that much fun and takes quite a bit of time.

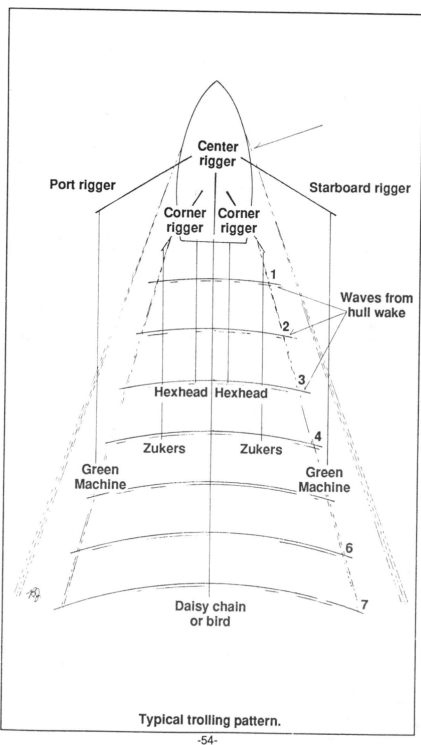

Port rigger

Starboard rigger

Center rigger

Corner rigger | Corner rigger

1

2

3

4

6

7

Waves from hull wake

Hexhead Hexhead

Zukers   Zukers

Green Machine

Green Machine

Daisy chain or bird

Typical trolling pattern.

Another common mistake, and I promise it's the last I'll discuss here, is that made by anglers trolling offshore who fail to recognize road signs that say "here's where the fish are." Those signs I call biological indicators which are discussed in Chapter Seven and serve to point the way to action. Time and again, boats and their crews seem to ignore these signs and leave the hot spot, trolling off to another area that might have been good days or weeks ago but now no longer holds bait, birds, fish, etc. Once you've found the fish, gotten a strike or two or three, work that area over again and again and again. It may be the only chance for action that day, so don't leave it until it dies.

In my program I show one particular slide that compares trolling success to swimming depth of the fish. The closer the fish are to the surface, the better your chances for a strike. Tuna, like other pelagic species, have a strike zone in which they will take a lure. This distance in which they will swim to take a lure varies due to conditions and it is basically conditions that control their swimming depth. For example, midday typically finds light intensity levels high with some tuna species swimming at deeper levels than others. With fish swimming at the 50 foot level, your chances of getting them up into your wake to strike a lure is poor. Whereas, if they are only 15 to 25 feet down, the chance of getting strikes is much better. Perhaps this is why early morning or late afternoon high speed trolling is much more successful.

Off and on, articles appear in various publications as to the proper pattern and spread for lures in the wake. However, what works for one boat may not work for another, depending on hull configuration, propulsion (single versus twins), trolling speed, wake configuration, outrigger placement and size, etc. I simply tell my audience what works for me and the underlying reasons it does.

There are a number of variations I make from a basic pattern, depending on species and conditions. I'll get to those in a moment, but, first, let's take a closer look. A seven line spread is easily done until there are very rough conditions. After that, the higher winds prevent line deployment and simply make it too uncomfortable to continue because of rough seas. As a general rule, if flat conditions exist, typical trolling speed of 6-7 knots can be bumped up to 7-8 knots and this seems to precipitate more strikes. With only a little wind, an additional set of flat lines at the corners and under the corner riggers set in the third or fourth wave can be fished with a total of nine lures in the wake behind the boat. As I'm sure you are beginning to realize, this becomes serious business.

Green Machines work best for me on the fifth wave for albacore and yellowfin. I'm convinced that the behavior of these fish, along with that of bigeye, is somewhat different from the other tunas in that these fish respond more to any surface disturbance, particularly that caused by the chine wake under flat conditions. On those days I'm convinced these species will travel great distances under a strengthening chine wake commotion, perhaps due to curiosity but, more probably, in the hopes of a meal. Coming up to the chine wake, the first lure they see is that on either the port or starboard outrigger. Perhaps this is why so many of my fish over the years have been caught on lures in this position behind the boat. If they were attracted to the propeller wake, my catch ratio would be higher on the other lines. But, I'm getting somewhat ahead of myself.

For high-speed trolling in the canyons with the potential of a large bigeye or billfish, the author uses only bent butt 80 or 130 pound outfits.

I use the center rigger on my boat to fish a bird rig or daisy chain of hard plastic back in the wake. It's only a guess, but I strongly suspect albacore or yellowfin when either, swimming at considerable depth or out a way laterally from the wake, zero in on the total commotion generated by both propeller and chine. By the time they zero in on the noise, the lures in front of them are those way back from the center rigger. On flat days I fish the lures way back in the ninth to eleventh waves. In fact, they are so far astern others new to offshore fishing might cut off the lines, thinking no one would have lures that far behind them. I can hear them laughing now – until a fish or two strike way, way back.

Birds or a chain of hard plastic lures might be better called attractors, not lures. In a bird rig, the lure follows about 24 to 32 inches behind the wing and is armed with a hook. The bird is simply a device that, in my opinion, attracts those distant or deeper swimming tuna, ones that would not normally be in the range to bite. Skittering across the surface, the bird sends up small jets of water that return as droplets, creating a commotion. I'd be willing to bet the bird produces sound frequencies that work to attract and excite, and immediately behind is the lure.

A few years back, when birds first made their appearance here, they were monsters. Designed and built for fishing the larger oceanic pelagics, it took an 80 or 130 pound outfit to tow them as they generated considerable pull. Smaller fish proved to be little or no sport in this heavy tackle.

My conversation with Captain Greg Metcalf, founder of Smoker Baits, convinced him there was a need for a smaller version of this concept and his product, designed with smaller wings, created much less drag and could be easily fished off a 30 or 50 pound outfit. In fact, for a while following their production, tackle shops serving the offshore fishermen were sold out of his product due to its popularity.

Back to lure placement. With good numbers of albies or small yellowfin, Zukers on the fourth wave will draw strikes if you keep it going (surging). Smoker Baits' Little Smokers will fish about as well with preferred colors a yellow/green combination, with the bright red/white/silver a close second. More about preferred colors later.

Over the years, some anglers have been surprised to learn that school bluefin tuna behave differently from similar sized albacore or yellowfin. These fish, destined to become giants by age ten, with a potential for living to more than 30 years of age (1,800 pounds), seem to gravitate toward the wake commotion produced by the propeller and move right under the third and second waves behind the transom. If you suspect that there may be small bluefin one to three years of age around, either a couple of Hexheads or small cedar jigs in this spot have a high potential for drawing strikes. More about preferred lures and the reasons why shortly. For whatever reasons, these young bluefin will sweep in deep under the boat for only a brief period of time before attacking these lures.

That aside, I must comment on an article that appeared recently in a noted offshore annual publication on lures for tuna. It was the opinion of the author that all tuna preferred a straight running lure. Well, I nearly choked and swallowed my bubble gum upon reading this malarkey, recognizing immediately that this individual had only little experience in the offshore scene.

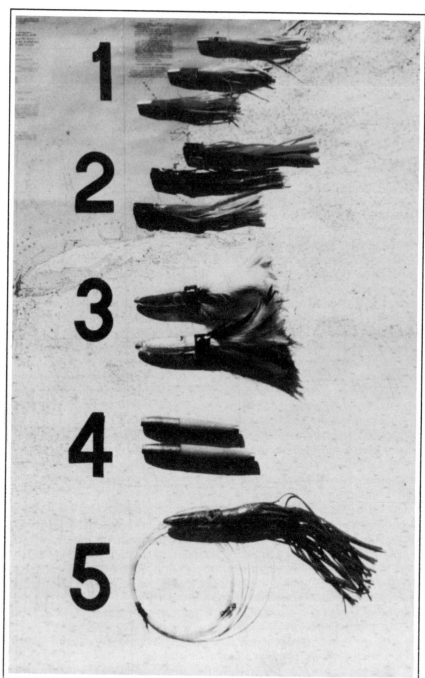

Selection of lures the author uses for smaller fish inside 40 fathoms. Top to bottom, they are: 1-Hexhead; 2-Little Smokers; 3-Sea Devils; 4-Cedar jigs; and 5-Green Machine.

When trolling for school bluefin tuna, the last thing you want to do is troll with rods in the holders or lines "in the clips" through an area that looks good. For reasons only little understood, a lure that is jigged or has built-in action, like a cedar jig, darting this way and that will draw strikes from these gamesters readily. For years my clients drew wraths like never before experienced if they didn't jig at the appropriate tempo or with the right sweep. Because of this, anglers on the *Prowler* have tagged and released more school bluefin tuna for the NMFS Cooperative Game Fish Tagging Program than any other boat in the history of this fisheries. The point is that school bluefin behave differently than young albacore or yellowfin. It's for the same reason that we'll have hooked and released several dozen or more Atlantic bonito as a result of jigging the feather in the fourth and fifth wave, while the rest of the fleet is struggling to make the day, as we say, trolling 'em "in the clips."

Years back, I had brought several lures popular in Florida back to New England for use offshore for tuna. With a little modification, I began to experience considerable success and they became pet lures. At that time, I had on the boat Captain Greg Metcalf who was then with Custom Mounts International which had plans to manufacture offshore trolling lures. With Greg in the cockpit, I dropped this lure prototype back into the wake, demonstrating how this modified lure smoked. With that, Smoker Baits was born and, following the company's production of that model, along with professional consultation, an arsenal of highly successful and affordable lures have become available.

Lure size, type and color are critical factors in the offshore trolling game, depending on the species sought. Perhaps more important is where those lures you have chosen are in the wake behind the boat. Every time I say this within earshot of Greg, he smiles, knowing full well my statement, "It's not only what you put into the water, it's where you put it." Right lures in the wrong place are no good; wrong size lures in the right place aren't any good either.

No doubt about it, the offshore angling fraternity favors certain basic colors, as do I. With the small feathers (three-quarter ounce), I prefer black and white or red and white. With HexHeads, orange and white or black and white. With those vinyl-skirted lured (Smokers, Zukers), the green and yellow combination seems to work the best, followed closely by red (hot pink) and white. Cedar jigs with a red head and white body, followed by the plain lead and wood natural color. All Eye lures from Striker and my vinyl-skirted lures are green and yellow or red and yellow. For the hard plastic chains, hot pink and lime green are my two favorite colors.

On more than one occasion I have taken a pair of scissors to a vinyl-skirted lure, trimmed it shorter, removed a few spacer beads (typically red), resulting in a higher frequency of bites. The size of the lure probably ranks second behind where you put it. Color is next in importance for those smaller tunas and bonitos.

A common technique used by many anglers is to increase the size of the lure as sea conditions roughen with the thought that it will be easier for the fish to spot, and to shorten the lines up a little and pull the throttle back slightly. You don't want the lures surging and jumping from the wave crests. Sea conditions dictate trolling speed and in flat conditions lines are com-

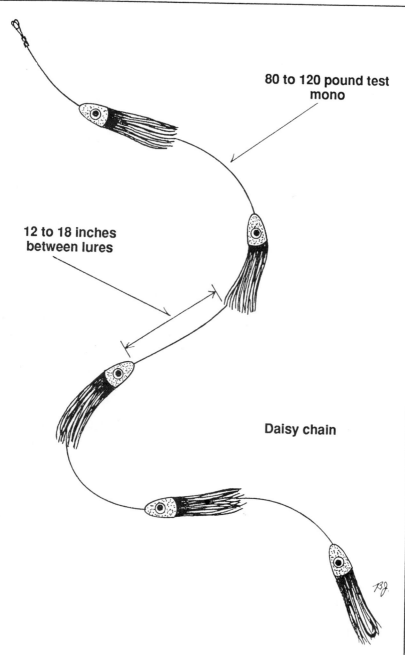

80 to 120 pound test mono

12 to 18 inches between lures

Daisy chain

Daisy chain of lures with hard plastic heads and vinyl skirts. There's usually 12 to 18 inches between each lure. The entire chain can be rigged with 80 to 200 pound mono but only the last lure has a hook in it.

monly lengthened somewhat and speed increased. You simply have to observe and note how particular lures fish under given conditions.

A few words now about the tackle that works best for me, and why. My arsenal of trolling tackle consists of custom-made rods with roller guides and tip top, and Penn International Series lever drag reels. These are loaded with either Ande or Berkley (Big Game) monofilament. Typically, the 50 pound class outfits are fishing out of the riggers and 30 pound class outfits are fishing the flat lines. In the canyon, with the potential for an overly large bigeye or yellowfin or even a sizeable billfish, only bent butt 80 pound class and 130 pound class outfits are employed. To make a long story short, I learned my lesson a long time ago – the hard way.

Now let's take a look at those lures commonly used inside of 40 fathoms for the smaller fish. Those lures identified as number 1 are called Hexheads, chrome plated, vinyl-skirted lures measure approximately six inches long and weigh about two ounces. This lure is typically fished straight to the hook (5/0 to 7/0 O'Shaughnessy Mustad #34007) on 30, 50 or 60 pound mono either clipped low at the transom or off the rod tip. An excellent lure, especially when jigged, it imitates those juvenile squid that both the tunas and bonito favor.

Next are the Little Smokers, measuring nearly seven inches in length and weighing about one ounce. This lure, too, is typically fished straight to the hook on mono up to 60 pound test. Depending on hook style and size, we use tribeads as spacers between the clinch knot at the hook and the hard plastic head. An excellent lure also, simulating those juvenile squid frequently preyed upon.

Number three is a lure no longer in production called the Sea Devil. It's a plastic headed and feathered lure measuring close to eight inches long and weighing about four ounces. Again, I fish these straight to a 7/0 or 9/0 hook on 80 pound test with colored tribeads as spacers. Simulating a squid, and fished back on the fifth, sixth or seventh wave, they draw savage strikes from longfin albacore.

Number four is the common cedar jig that employs a needle eye hook (Mustad #7731A or #7690) from 5/0 to 7/0 and is typically used with a single strand wire leader (#6 or #8). These lures can range in length from three to nine inches with the five and seven inch models weighing about five to six ounces the most popular. Fished back in the third wave behind the transom, darting and zig-zagging along, these lures have long been irresistable to school bluefin tuna up to 100 pounds or more.

Number five is the Green Machine, first offered years ago by Sevenstrand. This plastic headed, vinyl-skirted lure, approximately 12 inches in length and weighing about four ounces, has probably taken a wider range of pelagic species than any other high speed lure. Various manufacturers today offer similar style lures in a variety of colors. Because larger fish are more apt to take a swipe at it, it is typically fished on 100 to 200 pound mono leader with colored tribeads acting as a spacer between head and hook. The popular hook with this lure is a salmon style (Mustad #95160) in 7/0 to 9/0 sizes either tied or crimped in place.

My other favorite lures are saran and vinyl-skirted ones that I like to employ over and beyond the edge of the Continental Shelf, mainly for bigeye

Author's All Eye canyon lures are rigged with 250 pound mono, double crimped. They carry a pair of 10/0 Mustad hooks, model #7691S. A piece of 1,400 pound test, soft, stainless wire holds the trailing hook in place.

and yellowfin tuna. These are approximately 12 inches long with a flat face and large eyes. They are rigged on 250 pound test mono, double crimped, with a pair of 10/0 hooks (Mustad #7691S) in opposite positions with 1,400 pound test, soft, stainless wire holding the trailing hook in place. Rigged heavily, the rationale here is to have everything hold together as drag pressure elevates upward and over 55 to 70 pounds, particularly when several large fish are hooked simultaneously. Green and yellow and red and yellow are my preferred colors.

There is also a variety of lures called straight runners, differing not only in length and color but weight as well. As the sea state changes due to increasing wind, some prefer to use a heavier lure which fishes less erratically. Some of these lures weigh eight and ten ounces and others weigh 16 ounces to fish subsurface waters.

Last, but not least, is the typical hard plastic daisy chain made up of Little Smokers which could as easily be made up of soft plastics such as Moldcraft Squids. These are a series of lures one after the other with the last one having the hook. Most prefer to keep the colors constant, with the last lure and hook connected to heavy mono such as 150 pound test or more. Using either crimps or beads, or interspacing swivels, the intermediate lures are kept equidistant in their spacing. The variations on this theme are as different as those lures used to make them up.

There are usually "road signs" pointing to the location of offshore fish. Some days it's a very simple matter to locate the action.

CHAPTER SEVEN

Biological Indicators

Many afternoons, backing into the slip at the marina we found a sizeable crowd of summertime people peering into the cockpit to see what kind of luck we had. Frequently, the same person, perhaps one who may have been renting a vacation cottage for several weeks, indicated that we had a nice catch of tuna or bonito again, like the previous day. Or someone would ask how we managed to find the fish. Once in a while we had a little help from lady luck but, day after day? There's got to be something to it.

Even the most sophisticated equipment in the world might not help you find 'em if you don't know what to look for. I tell my customers and those folks on the dock that there are road signs out there pointing to the location of the fish and, on some days, it's a very simple matter to locate the action. And then there are the days when it's not quite so easy, when the weather or equipment create problems and the fish seem to disappear. One of the biggest reasons people take up offshore tuna fishing, in my opinion, is the challenge that comes in finding the fish. It's the anticipation or the hunt that gets us hooked on offshore tuna fishing. Okay, so what do we look for? Well, let's start with the obvious.

THE FISH

Tuna towers were developed to meet the need for seeing fish by looking down into the water and served another useful purpose by allowing one to see greater distances around the boat. To anyone who has ever been up in a tuna tower the perspective of the ocean changes significantly, allowing one to see things that are not readily visible from the cockpit level. Does that mean that to be a successful tuna/bonito fisherman you have to have a tower? Obviously no, but it sure helps. More importantly, the simple act of looking for fish can increase chances for success. Standing on the nonskid deck of a center console outboard powered boat cannot match the visual advantage of being 20 feet above the ocean's surface in a tuna tower. That doesn't mean you shouldn't be on the lookout for any signs of the fish themselves. For example, if you should recognize those V-shaped wakes made by fish swimming along just subsurface or that "bauble" created by a sizeable fish also just subsurface or the ruffled sea surface that looks like a puff of wind called a cat's paw but, in reality, are the wakes made by dozens of fish as they swim along just several feet under the surface. Sure, it's no trouble at all when jumpers come missiling out from the depths or when splashing fish can be seen on that crystal clear day. Boiling, feeding fish are tougher to see but the chances of getting a hook-up are better. In all cases, I prefer to take the trolled baits right to and through a body of fish on the surface with the hope that one or several will respond to the baits/lures in the wake of the boat. I prefer to slow troll those jumping yellowfin and bluefin in early season. Breaking, busting fish such as albacore and yellowfin a little later in the season usually jump on moments after you high speed troll over them. Likewise, with the bonito which, if schooled, require that you pass

Tuna towers allow a person to look down into the water and see farther around the boat.

directly over them. At the last moment, before they scatter into the depths, you run right over them, knowing full well you'll get that bite you've been waiting for.

THE BAIT

Unlike those white marlin that will ball a school of reddened squid, the tuna and bonito enjoy swimming headlong into this mass of potential food which, if near the surface, alert us to their behavior. They push their prey up against the "ceiling" in an attempt to reduce the dimensions in which they can possibly escape.

Typically, with clouds of sand eels in the water column come other animals like birds, whales, tuna, etc. A paper machine or color fish finder is a valuable tool for indicating the concentration of bait, where the fish are, etc.

There have been days when shoals of juvenile mackerel are being pushed up against the "ceiling," running above the surface in unison as tuna forage below. Certainly a sight to quicken one's pulse and an obvious biological indicator as to the presence of fish.

Trailing behind a dragger that has just hauled back for hundreds of yards can be juvenile whiting, hake, butterfish, etc. and, at times, these morsels are being picked off by bluefin of various sizes as well as yellowfin, These floaters, as they are sometimes called, can be easily gathered with a long handled dip net or landing net, providing one with enough bait for a serious attempt at a hook-up.

THE BIRDS

These are undoubtedly the strongest ally you have on the offshore grounds, providing you have decent visibility to spot them. True, they sometimes work over species other than tuna and bonito when far offshore (bluefish, marlin, etc.) but, then again, you're not going to ignore all those birds, are you? I sometimes refer to these feathered friends as action indicators and, by identifying what kind of bird and closely watching its behavior, I can sometimes get a pretty good idea of what's going on as we come into an area.

What kind of birds am I talking about? Birds that are ocean wanderers and those that are coastal, such as shearwaters, petrels, gulls, little gulls and terns. Get to know these animals and their behavior because they can tip the balance in your favor. Learn to recognize the signs between birds that are looking and those that are working. Birds that are rafted up in late morning usually indicate no need to cruise and soar as what they want and need are close at hand (bait fish). Those little gulls and terns that are hovering with rapid wing beat are probably staying over a few fish, easily seen at their height, waiting for the right moment to extract a morsel. Those Mother Carey's Chickens, or tuna birds or storm petrels are commonly seen working over a slick. A slick frequently arises from the depths due to fish (tuna) actively feeding. More than once I've saved the day by trolling back and forth, up and down through these slicks, finally locating a few fishes. And time and again I've come back inside 25 fathoms to find terns and little gulls working and chattering over a tide rip and weed line with fish feeding below.

Well, it's obvious, you say, with birds working, etc. that there must be a few fish around. Sure, that's why, time and again, I've watched particular boats make a pass or two and, surprisingly, move on. They didn't have a

Some mornings we steam right past a hotspot in an effort to get back to the hot numbers of the day before, only to realize our mistake later on.

strike so they left to look for another area with cooperating fish. Meanwhile, we're drilling the area. Five or six more passes without a strike and then, four fish on and finally, for me, the pressure is off.

Before I bring this discussion on birds to a close, let me confess that I, too, in the very early hours of daybreak, in an attempt to get right back out to a hotspot, went steaming right through all the birds and bait, thinking no way could all this life have moved this far in from outside during the hours of darkness. Yup, me, too; a victim of human nature, ignoring the most obvious signs and, arriving at yesterday's hotspot, finding it dead. Admitting stupidity, I raced back to those hastily jotted numbers on the console, praying that we might get back in time to catch a few fish, all the while, of course, knowing full well I almost blew it.

SLICKS

There are two basic kinds of slicks, those with and those without birds (storm petrels). I suppose some slicks are without birds because the birds haven't found them yet. At times, slicks give off a sweet, watermelon smell and others just a hint of what is going on down below. Slicks, of course, are very obvious when there is some wind smoothing the water like oil. Experts say this comes from prey species being caught, bit, chewed and swallowed. For whatever reasons, slicks can carry quite a distance down wind and current from the action which is why I prefer to work back up wind watching the fish finder very closely. One day last season, with only a few fish reported over the VHF radio at midday, it looked like a disaster was imminent. We had yet to have a bite. All of a sudden, or so it seemed, I recognized several slicks ahead. Back and forth, several times, not marking, and then we had three strikes, losing one fish almost immediately and boating two of the most lovely longfin albacore I have ever seen. We were the only boat with fish back at the dock that afternoon. Not great, but nevertheless success.

THE WHALES

Many scenes of whales (finbacks) come to mind when I look back at those successful days either chumming, slow trolling or diamond jigging. Other species, too, such as sei, humpback, pilot, etc., were present, all foraging on dense underwater clouds of sandeels with the tuna right in among them and birds working overhead. Although I can't prove it, it appears that in some way the feeding by these leviathans and that of medium/giant bluefin tuna can be interrelated at times. No one knows for sure exactly what goes on in the depths as these two widely different animals compete for food. One thing we know for sure is find the whales and you'll find the tuna.

Large yellowfins as well as bluefins are much less sensitive to temperature variations in the water column as they feed at considerable depths. Smaller, younger bluefin and yellowfin are sensitive to water temperature variations as small as 0.1°C and, hence, are not typically found in association with these large mammals.

Whether you have plans for slow trolling the chains or bars, chumming with herring, butterfish or mackerel, or diamond jigging the depths, finding the whales can be the first step in experiencing a successful day. With the whales, one typically finds the bait and, consequently, the fish.

THE JELLYFISH

Although the Gulf Stream carries a variety of jellyfish species to our

Finding the whales can be the first step in a successful trip. With the whales one typically finds the bait and the fish.

shores, perhaps the most noted and visible is the Portuguese man-of-war *(Physalia)*. This curious jellyfish, which is actually a whole colony of specialized individuals (noteworthy because of its nasty sting), has a "sail," often an iridescent blue, that is used to carry it along. Brought northward by the stream, they are associated with those warm core eddies that encroach upon the shelf. With them are tunas that live in these "bubbles" of blue water. As indicated earlier, these animals frequently indicate the nearby presence of water whose character (clarity, temperature, etc.) supports such tuna as yellowfin, bigeye and albacore.

THE SEAWEEDS

The seaweed that commonly indicates the presence of water whose character supports various tunas and bonitos is the Sargasso weed. This berrylike, yellow weed, which can serve to house a variety of sea creatures as it is carried along, frequently delineates major thermal gradients which control the presence of albacore, bigeye and yellowfin. Seen along major tide rips, it also signals the presence of a degrading warm core eddy. At times an annoyance as clumps of this weed become fouled on the hooks of our lures, it is readily tolerated. Unlike eel grass *(Zostera)*, this weed rarely puts a lure out of commission without our being aware of it.

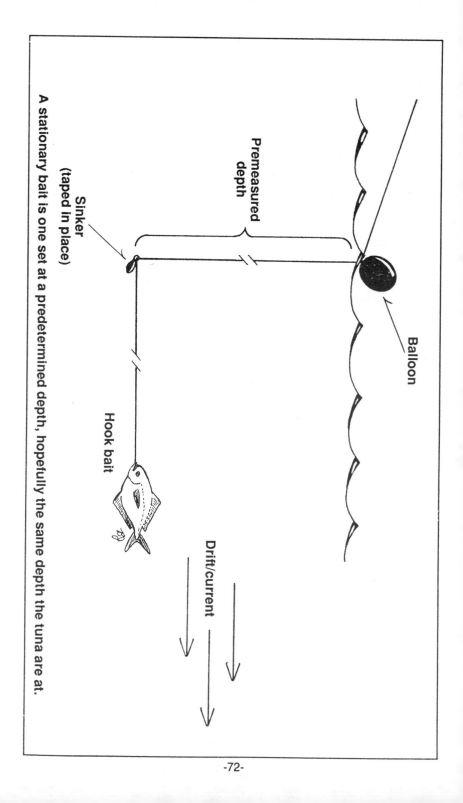

Balloon

Premeasured
depth

Sinker
(taped in place)

Hook bait

Drift/current

A stationary bait is one set at a predetermined depth, hopefully the same depth the tuna are at.

CHAPTER EIGHT

Chumming Techniques

If you have never stood at the transom, deliberately pulling line off a reel, allowing it to sink slowly along in the current after a carefully prepared hook bait, you simply can't appreciate the surge of excitement as the line is suddenly yanked from your gloved hands by a tuna. Whether setting the hook by hand or letting the reel do it as you quickly push the lever drag up, you've finally succeeded in getting that long awaited fish on.

This chapter, I hope, offers information to both the novice and the veteran tuna fisherman, explaining some of the basics involved in successful chumming for tuna.

Most of the chumming for tuna is done from an anchored boat, typically inside of 30 fathoms. Specialized anchor set ups are employed that allow for quick release from the anchor line as well as a marker buoy that is later used to assist with hauling the anchor from the depths. Precise anchoring techniques are a prerequisite for successful chumming, particularly when fishing in a fleet.

Chumming during the hours of darkness on the edge of the Continental Shelf usually involves tying up to lobster trawl gear and should only be done following permission from its owner and in a specific manner as dictated by the weather. Otherwise, one runs the risk of severe penalty should a complaint be made to the United States Coast Guard.

Whether in the canyon or on the near offshore grounds, chumming can also be done from a slowly drifting boat. Not a recommended technique when in a crowded fleet certainly, but, with little wind, scattered bait and fish, you'll have much less trouble and bother as a result of not having to handle the ground tackle. Should the wind come up, however, consideration should then be given to slipping the anchor overboard.

Swimming levels of the fish basically dictate whether to use a stationary bait or a free sinking bait. With giant bluefin marking at the 120 foot level, it makes sense to place a stationary bait there, whereas if you are watching the Atlantic bonito and false albacore flash through your chum line only 10 or 12 feet down, a free sinking hook bait will quickly draw those desired strikes.

Even the smallest outboard can easily fish two stationary lines with larger boats commonly fishing three or four. Basically, the hook bait is taken to a determined depth by a sinker and kept there by either a float or direct to the rod tip. The weight of the sinker used is determined by the size of the hook bait, depth at which it is fishing, diameter of the line, and velocity of the current. Lines that fish vertically seem to draw more strikes than those fishing at an oblique angle. A good number and selection of sinkers is necessary for success.

Actively chumming, but with no fish marking, it pays to fish at least one free sinking bait, allowing it to settle away in the chum line without any resistance. You do this by pulling line off the reel at a rate faster than the

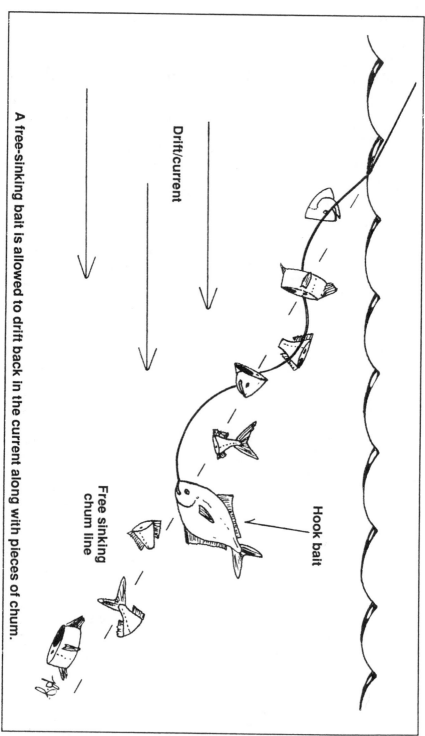

Drift/current

Hook bait

Free sinking chum line

A free-sinking bait is allowed to drift back in the current along with pieces of chum.

sinking rate of the bait, with a small amount (several feet) of slack in the water boatside.

A critical aspect of this technique is to carefully observe the sinking rate of the hook bait and match it to that of the cut chum. A large hook will cause the hook bait to sink out of the chum line, making it ineffective. A Styrofoam peanut inserted into the open end of the body cavity will offset this added weight and, with some playing around, you can adjust it accordingly. As a general rule, if you are marking fish in the upper levels of the water column, within 40 feet down, you have a good chance of getting a strike with a free sinking bait.

Whether fishing a stationary or sinking bait, lines that are premeasured and then marked at 50 foot intervals will greatly assist with the fishing. Typically, a series of half hitches of waxed nylon, like dental floss or dental tape, will allow you to get a bait to a specific level quickly, or let you know how much line is out on the chum line, and later on, with a fish on, allow you to evaluate the progress being made in the battle.

How do you hide the hook in the bait, either whole or cut? With a whole butterfish, for example, the point of the hook is inserted into the mouth, turning slightly, followed by the shank, which is then extracted from under and behind the gills. The leader or line now passes through the mouth and you hold the hook in your hand. Next, insert the point of the hook into the body cavity directly behind the gills, rotating and then pushing it backwards into the body cavity. This is easy to do with a small hook and a medium sized butterfish. Larger hooks require a jumbo sized butterfish if they are to fit inside the body cavity.

If chumming with herring, many prefer to cut off the head at an angle and, using a home-made wire tool, insert number 12 or 15 wire from the body cavity out through the center of the tail. The line or leader is then placed in the bend and pulled back through and the hook attached by means of a snell or clinch knot. Some prefer to allow the point of the hook to just pierce the skin as the hook snugs up in the muscle tissue behind the body cavity. With a large hook, a Styrofoam peanut can be used to offset its added weight. This technique can be used when putting a cut hook bait out as a free sinking bait. If spinning is a problem, the tail of the bait can be cut shorter with a knife on the chum board.

Commonly used bait, whether fresh or frozen, need not be the same as the hook bait. For example, you might be chumming with blueback herring and using a butterfish as a hook bait. Depending on cost and availability, the baits commonly used are mackerel, butterfish, herring and whiting.

Without a doubt, frozen butterfish are a much preferred chumming bait, shining like a silver dollar as the pieces settle away in the current set, along with creating only a minor mess on the cutting board. They are also much easier to cut than mackerel, herring or whiting.

Most experienced tuna fishermen will agree that using fresh bait is best, followed by frozen. If it's fresh frozen, that's nearly ideal, but watch for freezer burn or rancidity, undoubtedly affecting flavor and odor and, hence, behavior of those fish eating it. Fresh bait that is liberally packed in shaved ice will easily last several days in an onboard cooler. Fresh, clean ice in which to store your bait can be as important as the bait itself.

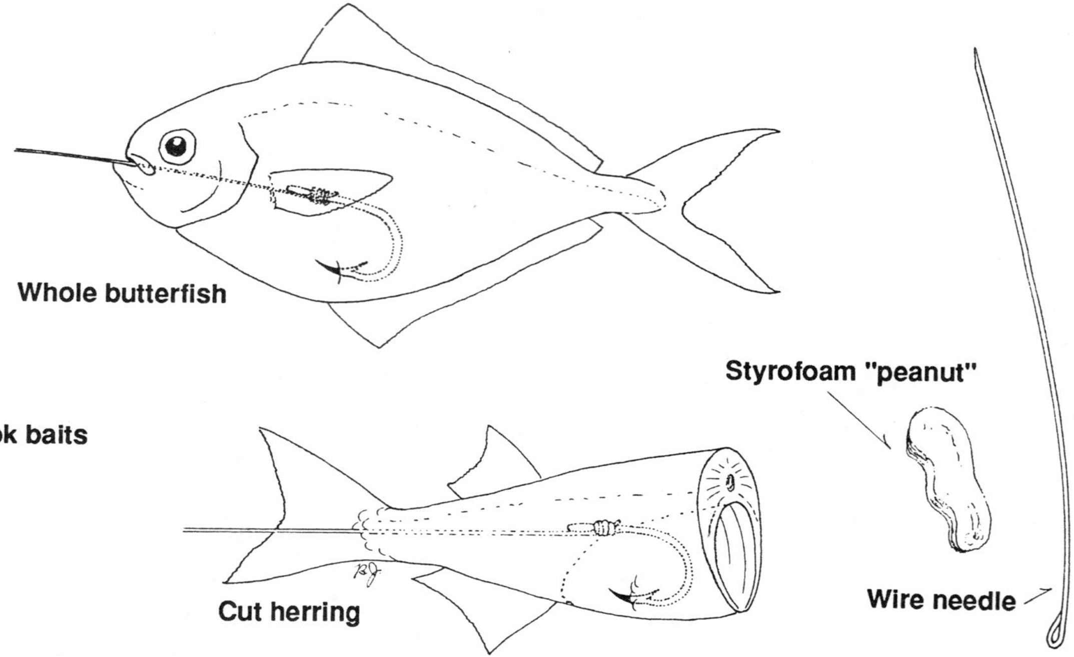

Whole butterfish

Typical hook baits

Cut herring

Styrofoam "peanut"

Wire needle

For butterfish, the hook is usually hidden inside the bait. When using herring, some anglers prefer to cut the head off, then, with a wire needle, insert the leader through the body cavity and out the tail. If a large hook is used, a Styrofoam peanut can be inserted in the bottom cavity to offset the hook's weight if herring is to be used as a free-sinking bait.

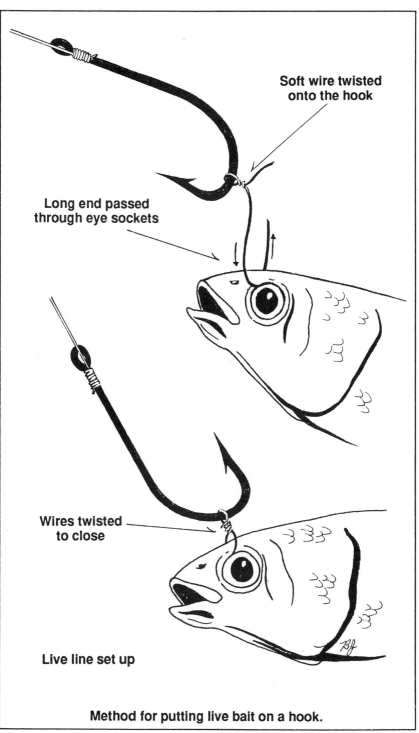

Soft wire twisted
onto the hook

Long end passed
through eye sockets

Wires twisted
to close

Live line set up

Method for putting live bait on a hook.

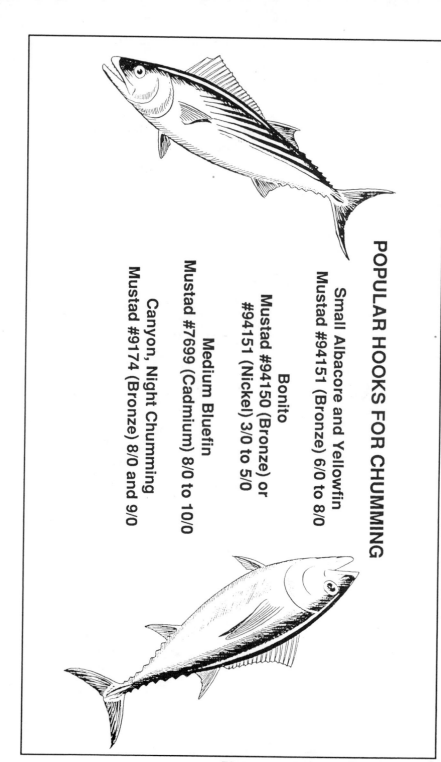

POPULAR HOOKS FOR CHUMMING

Small Albacore and Yellowfin
Mustad #94151 (Bronze) 6/0 to 8/0

Bonito
Mustad #94150 (Bronze) or
#94151 (Nickel) 3/0 to 5/0

Medium Bluefin
Mustad #7699 (Cadmium) 8/0 to 10/0

Canyon, Night Chumming
Mustad #9174 (Bronze) 8/0 and 9/0

Occasionally, good supplies of suitable hook baits become available and, because of sporadic availability during the season, could be packaged and frozen for later use. Putting several packages with a half dozen hook baits, double bagged (Ziplock) and dated, away in a freezer will assure you of a choice at a later time. Culling through a tote of fresh bait may or may not offer a good number of suitable hook baits. With one or two packages of fresh frozen along on the ice, you've got the bait should the bite turn hot. Appearance and freshness, as well as size, are important factors in getting a bite on your carefully chosen hook bait.

Few will argue when you state that the deadliest combination for success is a live bait swimming in a chum line at the right level. Snapper blues, tinker and adult mackerel and whiting jigged off the bottom have affected a deadly toll on both bluefin and yellowfin. There are, however, lots of problems involved in securing a number of suitable live baits, transporting them to the grounds, keeping them alive and spunky, and then getting them on the hook and to a level in which the tuna are swimming. Handling the bait can result in initial levels of stress that are compounded by high water temperature and lowered oxygen levels of the holding container. It's best to catch the live bait, if possible, on or near the tuna grounds.

How do you go about putting them on the hook? Several methods are preferred in order to prolong the life of the bait. An 8 to 10 inch section of soft wire, twisted several times around the bend of the hook can then be inserted in the eye socket, either in front of or behind the eye of the bait, through the bony skull and out the other eye socket. Drawing close to the hook, additional twists are made, quickly snipped, and the bait is overboard without too much trauma. Others prefer to run the wire through the back well away from the backbone, relying only on skin and muscle to hold the bait to the hook. The key to success is placing it at the swimming level of the fish. That's why it pays to have someone on board constantly watching the fish finder, noting the fish and their swimming depth.

Over the years I've noticed subtle differences in the behavior of the various tunas and bonitos when in the chum slick and, if possible, I try to adjust my techniques accordingly. For example, I have a very difficult time getting longfin albacore to take a stationary bait, but, when under the boat and back in the chum line, they will readily take a free sinking bait. Likewise, those Atlantic bonito that zip through the slick and line of settling bait. Not so with bluefin tuna that will quickly take a stationary bait, providing it looks good. Large yellowfin tuna will also take a stationary bait, particularly when feeding at a considerable depth. However, in the upper levels of the water column, they become much more cautious, except at night. All of the tunas and bonito will readily take a free sinking bait in the chum slick, providing it looks natural. Of course, I can only guess at the reasons for these behavioral differences, but I think it's related to swimming speed and visual acuity.

What's the best way to chum? Well, I've been telling my customers for years that anchored up in a fleet of boats and marking fish 80 or 100 or more feet down is a waste of time, money and effort to chum. By the time our bait reaches those levels, it's probably well over several hundred yards away. Best bet is simply to put out baits (stationary) at those levels in which the fish are marking.

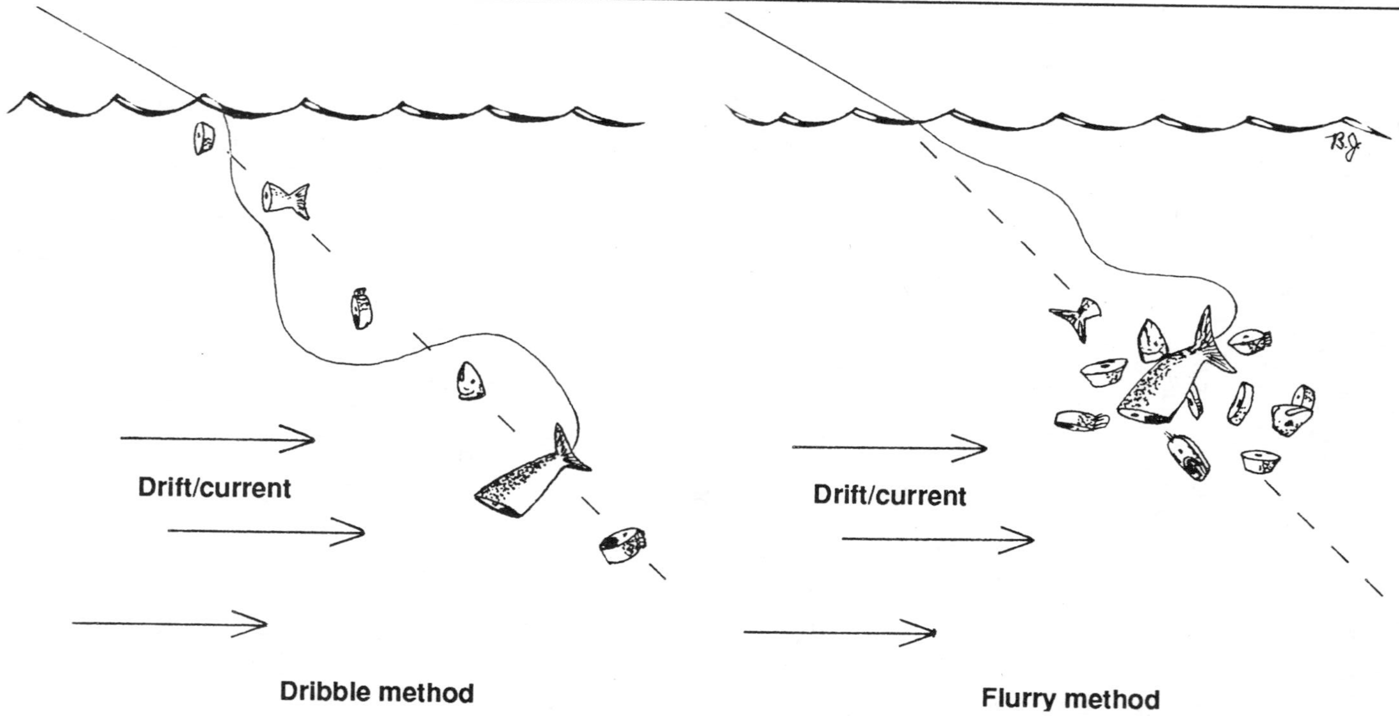

Drift/current

Dribble method

Drift/current

Flurry method

The dribble method of chumming utilizes small amounts of chum dropped overboard at intervals. Using the flurry method, an angler dumps a "cloud" of cut bait over the side all at once with a hook bait presented in the middle of the cloud.

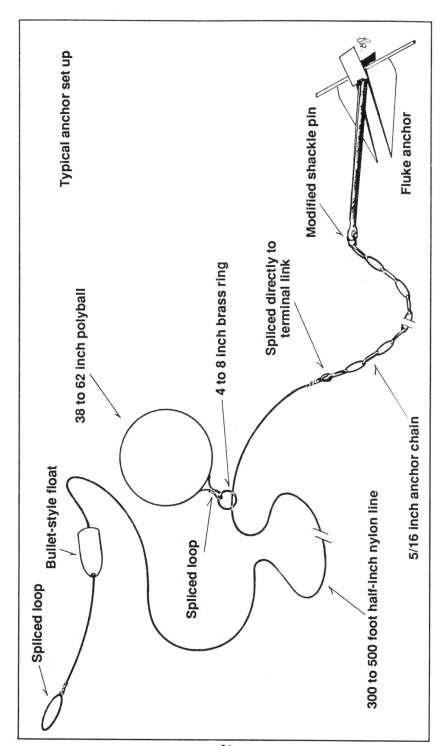

Typical anchor set up

Spliced loop

Bullet-style float

38 to 62 inch polyball

4 to 8 inch brass ring

Spliced directly to terminal link

Modified shackle pin

Fluke anchor

Spliced loop

5/16 inch anchor chain

300 to 500 foot half-inch nylon line

On the other hand, if we suspect there are fish in the upper levels of the water column, we can either put a stationary bait out or start a chum slick and fish a free sinking bait or both. Now you have to decide on either the dribble method or the flurry method of chumming. In the dribble method, several pieces, one behind the other, are tossed overboard and, when they can no longer be seen, several more pieces are dribbled overboard. The idea is to entice them, not to feed them. Over-chumming can lead to the fish hanging way back in the chum line and gorging themselves. You then run the free sinking bait back and out 200 feet and then retrieve. If the sinking rate is one foot for every five feet in the current, you have reached the 40 foot depth. Then, you do it all over again, pulling slack once more as the bait continues to sink away in the current set.

In the flurry method, the concept is to toss several handfuls of cut chum overboard with your hook squarely in the center of it all. The commonly held idea is that as this cloud of cut bait descends, it not only is highly visible but may attract several fish simultaneously that will compete for that larger piece, your hook bait. This competition may precipitate a strike even though appearances aren't quite natural, as if a cloud of cut bait could ever be considered such! If there are no bites, the hook bait is retrieved, several more handfuls acquired, and the process repeated all over again.

With either method, some prefer to ladle over a soupy mixture of ground up chum (shark chum) and toss in an occasional sandeel to spice things up. Many feel the presence of small bait like juvenile mackerel works to excite these larger predators, and the added chum certainly can't hurt.

Over the years there have been those times when the fish bite readily on our hooks. Only problem was they were the wrong kind of fish (bluefish, dogfish). What do you do in a case like that? Move to another spot and, before too long, you're bothered again. On many days, they are only a temporary nuisance but, other days, a disaster as the numbers of these fish overwhelm the tuna and, because of shear numbers, prevent a tuna bite. It's these days when you better have a very good supply of Maalox as well as hooks, leader and line aboard if you intend to fish through them, not to mention an adequate supply of hook baits. If so, you better treat each and every bite as a tuna bite or you could be taken unawares and not prepared for that tuna you're working for.

Finishing up this discussion on chumming, a few years of experience have fostered some changes to the typical anchor setup employed on the grounds. The spliced loop at the bitter end allows for a quick release or easy attachment to a cleat, as well as preventing the bullet float from coming off. This, in turn, keeps the polyball from coming off if cast loose. Whether a 300 or 500 foot length of one-half inch nylon, it carries an eight inch ring connected to a polyball with the boat's name on it. The opposite end is spliced directly to the terminal link of the chain, allowing the ring to run to the anchor shank. Even the shackle pin end is ground down to allow the ball/ring to travel to the shank of this Danforth style anchor, floating it neatly after having run down its length.

CHAPTER NINE

Behavior Patterns

My guess is that many readers will turn to this chapter first although each of the chapters in this book profiles some of the behavior demonstrated by several or all of those species considered. This discussion focuses on what I believe are common behavior patterns as well as some species differences, a few of which have already been considered or will be before the end page. The basis for each description is the result of considerable experience and common sense, honed by many, many hours of observation while in pursuit of these wonderful and exciting animals. Perhaps, as a result of this effort, you, too, can get a somewhat better insight into their behavior, with consequent better angling success. That tuna/bonito do behave in a certain fashion is for sure, but why it happens can only be answered by scientific endeavors. With casual reading of the scientific literature, I can now report that some of those reasons have become well documented.

TURBULENCE ATTRACTION — Propeller Noise

Of all of those species considered herein, none demonstrates a stronger affinity for propeller wash than does a juvenile, one to three year old, 8 to 45 pound, school bluefin tuna. The young of this species quickly orient themselves under the second, third or fourth wave behind the transom in the white water wake of the boat. Years ago, those routinely fishing for school tuna, and enjoying success at it, had fun with other fishermen by telling them their success was due to a chromed propeller or a metal trash can cover trolled, tumbling and splashing back in the wake. Actually, it was due in part to their knowledge of where in the wake these fish would briefly orient themselves. Propeller noise apparently attracts these fish more so than any other we are familiar with. Since we do not routinely see juvenile bigeye tuna or albacore, we have little or no chance for comparison, although they, too, may behave in the same fashion. Be that as it may, we put our feathers, cedar jigs and Hexheads in the third and fourth waves behind the boat if we suspect school bluefin tuna are around and set those Green Machines on the fifth wave for other tuna species.

TURBULENCE ATTRACTION — Chine Wake Noise

Disturbing the surface of the ocean with a fast trolling boat or spraying water on it from a high pressure/volume pump and hose creates an attraction irresistible to tuna. Turbulence, like that from a chine wake, attracts and excites members of the tuna tribe. Perhaps, as experts suggest, it mimics a feeding spree in progress, with a chance for a meal should they be on the scene. It appears the sound created by a moving boat, particularly that of a chine wake on the surface, is readily investigated by larger members of the tuna clan. Drawn in by the overall boat and propeller noise, a yellowfin tuna may travel hundreds of yards under a strengthening chine wake, becoming, as a guess, more excited in the process as it closes to the boat. Approaching the wake, the first lures readily obvious are those fishing off either the port

A yellowfin may travel hundreds of yards under a strengthening chine wake, becoming more excited as it closes to the boat.

or starboard outrigger and, consequently, these are most frequently attacked. If properly placed, splashing along just inside the chine wake, but outside the hull wake, lures in such a position in this narrow corridor of calmer water seem to draw almost immediate attention. Other fish, deep and lateral to the passage of the boat, drawn in by the commotion, also see those lures on the outboard riggers first. As a result, lures here account for the highest number of single fish.

TURBULENCE ATTRACTION —Bird Rig

A single fish, no longer a member in a school, drawn upwards from the depths by the overall boat noise, that senses a bird rig commotion, may be triggered into striking the trailing lure as a result. This is an effective lure when fished way back, particularly under oily, calm surface conditions, suggesting that surface noise is indeed strongly influencing their feeding behavior. In my opinion, bird rigs should be called attractors, not lures. Actually, the lure follows about 24 to 40 inches behind the bird and is armed with the hook. Skittering across the surface, the bird sends up small jets of water that return as droplets, creating a commotion. Perhaps curiosity turns into aggressive feeding behavior once the trailing lure is recognized as a potential meal.

STRIKE THRESHOLD LEVELS — High Speed Surging

One of the techniques employed for creating a multiple high speed trolling hookup, effective on bigeye, yellowfin and albacore, is one called surging. With the first fish on, perhaps one of many in a school, the throttle(s) is/are pulled back somewhat then pushed up, pulled back, etc., repeated two or three more times over a period of 15 to 25 seconds. This technique can be enhanced by simultaneously turning the boat slightly right and then left, which speeds up the outboard (turning radius) lures and slows down the inboard (turning radius) lures. Perhaps it's the changing sound levels and changing speed of the lures that lowers the threshold for striking by other members of this same school. That it works is fact, but why is still up to conjecture. With that third or fourth or more fish on, the throttle(s) can then be brought back down to idle speed in gear and pressure put on. With this procedure, obviously, attention must be paid so as not to dump that first reel or two.

STRIKE THRESHOLD LEVELS — High Speed Jigging (Trolling)

With both school bluefin and Atlantic bonito, as well as other members of the bonito tribe, jigging of the trolling rods is another highly effective technique for creating those multiple hookups. For whatever reasons, these fish obviously perceive a jigged lure as the one to engulf. Straight running (unjigged) lures simply do not get the same attention as those darting, zigging and zagging in the wake behind the boat. Experts tell us this action imitates an injured bait (squid) and, therefore, one that is easily consumed. Whatever the reason, this is an effective technique. Could it be that these fish are quicker to focus on an erratic swimming lure, whose silhouette against the surface is somewhat hidden in the shadows of the surface bubbles in the wake? Perhaps an erratic swimming lure does represent a badly injured prey and is the reason surging is also an effective technique. Jigging a trolled lure is an art/skill only a few anglers pick up quickly, but it can be readily mastered with a little practice.

Multiple hookups with albacore are possible with a technique called surging.

AVOIDANCE BEHAVIOR —Vertical (Stationary) Lines

Lots of anglers set their stationary lines (baits on a float) out in the chum slick with the deepest line being that most distant, with the thought that the cut chum will be deeper in the water further away from the boat as it settles. Stationary lines are then set to match nearly the levels of the sinking bait, with hopes that a fish moving up the chum line will see and bite on the offered hook bait. Certainly this is a valid concept and one that works when numbers of fish and feeding competition is high. But, with fewer fish and reduced competition in the chum line, perhaps these same fish become less aggressive, more cautious and deliberately avoid those areas around the up and down lines. The bait and leaders of the two shallow lines, if close to a vertical line, may readily prompt the fish to avoid that area or shy away, with the result being no bites.

On the other hand, by fishing bass-ackwards with the closest line deepest and the furthest lines shallow, an avoidance response by the fish to a vertical line is eliminated. Because vertical lines tend to converge in the current away from the boat, they have the potential to be quite close to one another. In any case, you might want to consider bait deployment in this fashion should you not be experiencing full action potential.

AVOIDANCE BEHAVIOR — Line Drag

Heavy diameter lines and leaders that drag along on the ocean surface immediately in front of the offered bait or lure can create another avoidance behavior. Highly significant when slow speed trolling, less so when in the high speed trolling mode, as the resulting white water (bubbles) tends to hide better (shadows) those lines attached to offerings. Keep in mind that these fish have keen vision and that lines, leaders, snaps, swivels, etc. that create surface commotion can and do result in fewer strikes. Line elevation when using heavy lines and leaders during calm conditions can help eliminate this particular tuna behavior problem.

JUMPING BEHAVIOR

Early in the season, watching those larger yellowfin tuna clearing the surface of the ocean as they jump for no apparent reason, creates amazement and prompts the question as to why. Like bluefin tuna, this species also develops thermoregulatory ability, but to a lesser degree, and biologists today think that jumping is a behavior mechanism that serves to elevate blood and body tissue temperatures. The high speed swimming bursts that jumping requires generate considerable body heat from muscle contraction, triggered, perhaps, by low body core temperature. We do know that larger adults and those of bigeye tuna as well can invade somewhat colder food-rich waters than that tolerated by juvenile members of the same species. With a counter current, heat vascular exchange system, these larger yellowfin can invade the colder, deeper levels of the water column. However, small yellowfin, like small bluefin, have yet to develop the ability to thermoregulate and, hence, are limited in their distribution to the warmer, upper levels of the water column. Perhaps for this reason we do not typically find them in the same depths as giant bluefin and why they cannot invade the normally colder waters of the Gulf of Maine. By the time bluefins attain giant size, however, they can easily swim in the colder waters of the Canadian Maritimes in search of food. Perhaps if yellowfin tuna grew to the size of bluefins they, too, could survive in much colder waters. Studies have shown that young yellowfin are sensitive to as little as 0.10°C difference in sea temperature. Although jumping yellowfins raise frustration levels significantly, there has been some success attained by slow speed trolling through areas of this activity.

SCHOOLING BEHAVIOR

All species of tuna and bonito, like other fishes, demonstrate various levels of schooling behavior but, among them, that of the bluefin appears to be the strongest, not just with juveniles, but adult fish as well. A few years back, with a giant bluefin on, I could easily look down into the water column from my controls in the tower. As I watched, I could see six other fish of similar size swimming along with the one hooked. Angler and crew had fits as the line connecting the rod and fish jumped, a result of the other giant bluefin swimming along and into our line early in the battle. However, as the battle progressed, these other fish disappeared.

With school bluefin, if you have one on behind the boat, there can be dozens of others following along and behind. This simply doesn't happen with albacore or yellowfin. Atlantic bonito also will school along with a hooked fish but much deeper and further behind.

This intense schooling behavior by young bluefin has been recognized by trollers for years and has enabled them to load up by deep jigging once a fish was hooked. Often fish were caught till arms ached or line parted as a result of tightening the drag due to fatigue overcoming any thoughts of sport.

SWIMMING BEHAVIOR — Swimming Levels

Several factors appear to affect swimming levels of the various tuna/bonito species, among them water temperature, light intensity and dissolved oxygen levels, not necessarily in that order. As many are aware, these fish are typically near the surface during periods of low light intensity and, then, move deeper in the water during periods of high light intensity, except for the bonito, which typically appear to be unable to tolerate the colder waters beneath a thermocline. Recent research indicates both yellowfin and bigeye tuna swim closer to the surface at night, possibly to reduce body temperature loss to the surrounding water as near surface water is the warmest. Others believe it to be for foraging (feeding) on creatures such as squid that typically rise to near surface levels at night. Research has indicated that dissolved oxygen levels may also be a limiting factor in the vertical distribution of bigeye and yellowfin tuna. However, since most readers will limit their hook and line fishing to less than 100 meters below the ocean surface, dissolved oxygen is of little significance. Research on the pineal gland of tunas suggests that at least one species responds to high light intensity by moving into the depths, returning to near surface levels as daylight diminishes.

SWIMMING BEHAVIOR — Pushing Fish

Once we recognize that either bonito or small bluefin are swimming along just subsurface (pushing), we typically attempt a high speed trolling pass over them with hopes for multiple strikes. From the tower, only moments before actually going over the school, we see them break away en masse toward the depths, disappearing beneath the chine and propeller wake. However, these smaller fish will quickly gravitate back near the surface in the wake of the boat. If we have small lures back in the third, fourth and fifth waves, frequently we get a bite or two. Best chances for success are to troll over the fish in a quartering fashion, in a near direction to which they are swimming. Poor results come when running over them head on. Perhaps being opposite to the general direction in which they are traveling causes these fish to scatter further and deeper. With larger fish, the best approach is to get up ahead of them and then angle in toward the lead fish with trailing baits or lures. If spooked, the larger fish, too, will scatter into the depths and, for whatever reasons, appear not to reschool as quickly as their younger brothers. Perhaps it is because these larger fish are more tolerant of the cooler depths, where they can remain for a longer period of time.

SWIMMING BEHAVIOR — Local Occurrence

The haphazard movements of bait along with the whims of local weather will affect the distribution of a body of fish, but, perhaps most important, is that of local water temperature. As discussed in previous chapters, late summer and early fall low pressure atmospheric systems and accompanying winds tend to drive local tuna and bonito into deeper, warmer waters. Large bluefin and yellowfin tuna seem to move less quickly, probably as a result of their being more tolerant to cooler waters. Being visual predators, they, too, depart as surface waters lose both their clarity and warmth.

Small fish like albacore appear to move off in a nearly downwind direction, perhaps because it is the shortest distance to deeper, warmer water. But, then again, anyone with some offshore fishing experience is quick to recognize the swimming behavior of tunas and billfishes as it related to wind and wave direction. Wind-driven waves contain energy and these fish have long used that energy to assist them in their swimming behavior.

As a general rule, with a major late season storm, small yellowfin are the first to go, closely followed by albacore. Oceanic bonito, if around, follow suit. Small bluefin linger longer, being slightly more temperature tolerant. Should high bait concentrations persist, medium and giant bluefin, along with false albacore and its cousin the Atlantic bonito, can persist well into late season (November). Once the offshore waters cool, only extended periods of settled weather may see the return of tuna and then, notably, only the bluefin. Typically, species like yellowfin, albacore, oceanic bonito, etc. are gone for the season.

FEEDING BEHAVIOR — Conditions

Ask anyone with surf fishing experience for striped bass what calm surf conditions do for the fishing. But, let conditions change to waves and white water, and, suddenly, things become different. Now these fish will aggressively hit your offered tin squid, jig or plug. Tuna and bonito behave in nearly the same fashion as well, biting, as a rule, with reckless abandon as the sea state roughens. But, then, when conditions become too rough, you are forced to modify boat speed, lure presentation, trolling direction (in the trough versus into the sea), lure size, etc. No doubt about it, as sea state changes, so, too, does the behavior of these fish. Typically, they become more aggressive with increased amounts of white water, particularly after a prolonged period of settled weather. When I tell clients that the direction of the wind is going to influence their day's success, I get a funny look. They ask, "How do the fish know the direction the wind is blowing when swimming deep in the ocean?" Plain and simple: they do, but don't ask me how!

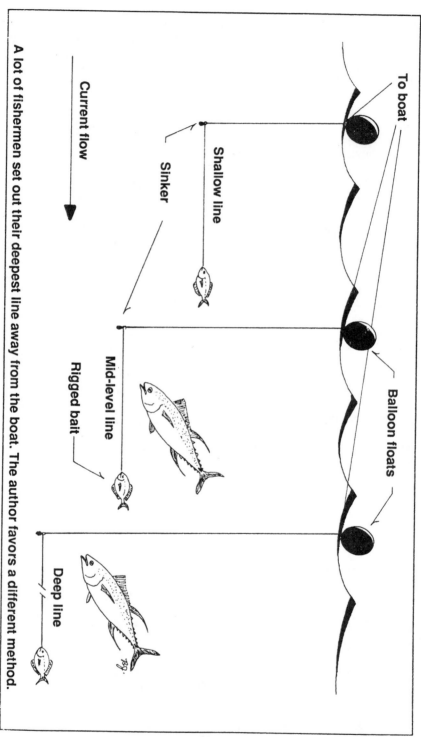

To boat

Current flow

Shallow line

Sinker

Mid-level line

Rigged bait

Balloon floats

Deep line

A lot of fishermen set out their deepest line away from the boat. The author favors a different method.

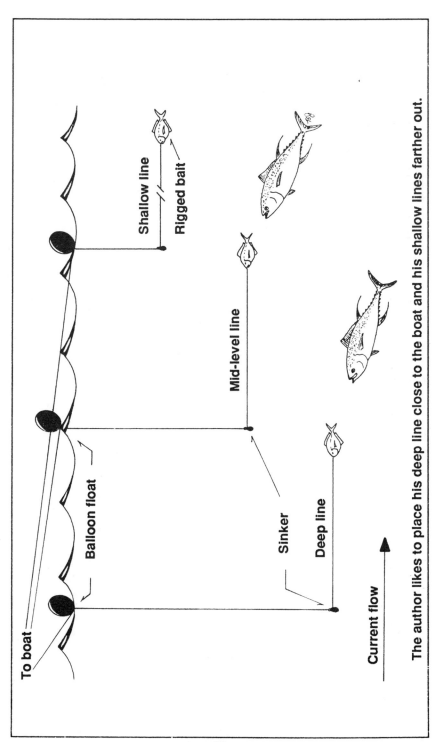

The author likes to place his deep line close to the boat and his shallow lines farther out.

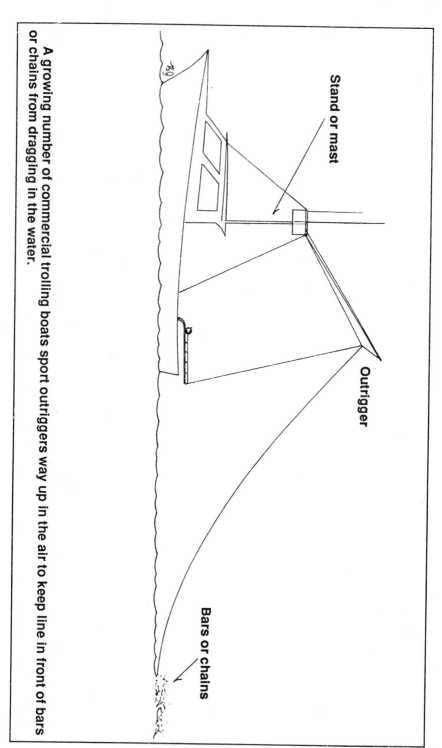

Stand or mast

Outrigger

Bars or chains

A growing number of commercial trolling boats sport outriggers way up in the air to keep line in front of bars or chains from dragging in the water.

FEEDING BEHAVIOR — Surface Levels

The open ocean usually allows prey to flee from their predators through three dimensions, left versus right, forward versus backwards, up versus down. In an attempt to reduce the chances for escape, tuna, like other predators, frequently force their prey up "against the ceiling" or ocean surface. This eliminates one of those potential dimensions for escape. With busting fish on the surface, their presence is readily obvious, whereas deep feeding behavior could easily go unnoticed were it not for that tell-tale slick formation on the surface.

During those times tuna and bonito have their prey up against the ceiling, they appear to lose much of their cautiousness, perhaps because surface conditions interfere with visual acuity and/or feeding simply excites them. For whatever reasons, they will strike readily at surface lures nearby. Under these conditions, slow trolling for larger fish allows you to present a large sized bait or lure for an extended period of time in the strike zone. On the other hand, high speed trolling with smaller lures seems to be more effective on the smaller fish.

FEEDING BEHAVIOR —Deeper Levels

As many experienced anglers will agree, some species of tuna behave differently than others when feeding in the depths. When comparing a free sinking bait to a stationary one, one might expect only little difference in effectiveness. Not so, as many have considerable trouble during daylight hours in getting albacore to bite a stationary bait, even with the lightest of lines; likewise those Atlantic bonito that congregate behind the boat in a chum line. However, both of these fish will readily take a free sinking bait in the upper levels of the water column. This technique simply seems to work better for those species. I suspect that the typically higher swimming speeds of these fish, when in the chum slick, have something to do with this behavioral difference. On the other hand, bluefin tuna appear to take a stationary bait more readily than other species. I think it can be safely said that any of those tuna and bonito that venture into a chum slick can be enticed into taking a free sinking bait, assuming light line, small hook and fresh bait.

FEEDING BEHAVIOR — In the Slick

As indicated in the previous chapter, at times the trick of the flurry method of chumming will get the bite you are looking for. Watching fish as they swim through the chum line from cockpit levels can't frequently be done, but, over the years, it became obvious that feeding tuna and bonito can be very selective in their taking of cut pieces. Competition among those fish in the chum line may become intensified with the flurry method. As this large cloud of cut pieces descends, visually attracting good numbers of feeding fish, they may become more aggressive and less selective, with your hook bait and its obvious leader the first to go. However, in the process of looking at stomach contents over the years, I gather quite a bit of interesting information suggesting that fish can be selective. One fish had only midbody cuts of herring while another fish taken that same day had tail sections predominating. But, most memorable, was one particular giant bluefin tuna that had just pogy (menhaden) and whiting heads in its stomach. Heads sink faster and, hence, get to feeding depths quicker.

Perhaps if yellowfin grew to the size of bluefins they, too, could survive in much colder waters.

FEEDING BEHAVIOR — Memory

Recent investigations suggest that several tuna species possess memory, that is they demonstrate the repeated behavior of swimming back to a particular site on a daily basis. Pacific yellowfin tuna have demonstrated the ability to learn the position of a FAD (Fish Aggregating Device) in Hawaiian waters by navigating to and from them even when widely separated)over 10 nautical miles). Because of their fish-attracting ability, these Hawaiian deep water buoys have come to play an important role, as have other buoys worldwide, in both a recreational as well as a commercial fishery. Is there a possibility that our canyon yellowfin, bigeye and albacore use those buoys and lines of the lobster trawls in much the same fashion for temporary periods of time? Those familiar with this canyon fishery agree the trawl lines and buoys seem to attract fish closer to the surface, much like those FADs of the Pacific. Could it be these fish find their way back on a daily basis, resulting in that hot bite for several nights running on a particular ball when conditions are favorable? Yellowfin tuna have the ability to navigate to precise areas on the globe's surface as a result of their being sensitive to the electromagnetic fields of our planet, much like that of the compass card in front of your helm. Why is it that chumming fleets seem to develop on similar numbers season after season? True, aggregations of bait tend to develop along contour lines, which are frequently traveled by tunas. Perhaps it's more than just coincidence when we see on-going action for weeks at a time in a given area. Few of us may only recognize short term memory (tuna) even when demonstrated right in front of our faces!

FIGHTING BEHAVIOR — Light Tackle

Countless times, over the years, anglers aboard the *Prowler* have attempted to take fish on light tackle, often times succeeding, with a resulting lesson in tuna behavior. With light drag pressure, initial struggles quickly result in the fish coming to the surface where it then attempts to conduct sustained near surface swimming. If new to this fishing and you have a fish on that has been near the surface for extended periods, you simply are not exerting enough pressure on the fish to tire it quickly. With only light drag pressure, you will spend considerable time chasing after the fish. Good luck!

FIGHTING BEHAVIOR — Heavy Tackle

A tuna or bonito having relatively heavy drag pressure applied to it initially will typically make for the depths. Only after developing high levels of tissue hypoxia (oxygen debt) will it change tactics, coming to the surface and then going deep again. With ensuing fatigue, it can no longer maintain an upright orientation and will begin to succumb to line pressure by laying over. This results in a circling swimming motion, your first indication of a tiring fish. If you can create a slight heads-up attitude by pumping the rod, the fish will swim itself in circles toward the surface. However, just because a fish allows itself to get pumped to the surface doesn't mean it's whipped. A knowledgeable crew knows full well that until a fish can be lead nose first by pulling on the leader, it is not fully exhausted. Green fish at boatside are at high risk for loss. The taking or tagging of a fish is best done when it can be easily maneuvered along side.

Line manufacturers began providing black dacron and, at the same time, high quality monofilament line in heavier pound tests became available.

CHAPTER TEN

Visual Acuity

Newcomers to offshore tuna fishing may not be aware of the evolution that has taken place in recent years with regard to lines, leaders, and, to some extent, hooks, most notable with bluefin tuna, particularly as a result of their becoming so valuable on the Japanese export market. With a strong profit motive as the reason to go giant tuna fishing, terminal tackle underwent a rapid evolution. So, too, did other equipment like bent butt rods and lever drag reels.

All of this was a result of anglers creating a need and recognizing these fish can see very well. Their visual acuity was superior to that of most inshore species and, as a result, took a bit more finesse to get on the line. Unlike codfish, which could be taken on tarred line straight to the hook, or bluefish that would savagely take a plug behind a nylon-coated leader, crude terminal tackle for tuna often times simply failed to work.

Braided dacron line was in vogue in the early 1970s for use on larger fish and, being typically white in color, stood out like a neon sign in the water column. When the line was darkened with a felt marker or dyed black, the bites came quickly. Soon the line manufacturers were providing black colored dacron and, at the same time, high quality monofilament line in heavier pound tests became available. This offered a definite advantage at times and is highly favored today on the offshore scene. Dacron still has a place, but strictly for giant bluefin tuna.

Leader material also underwent a rapid evolution, from heavy, braided or twisted aircraft cable to single strand, coffee colored, stainless wire to monofilament. Some anglers tie the hook right to the mono, gambling on a hinge-hooked fish or the prearranged antichafing gear doing its job.

Hooks also played an important role in successful fishing with the smaller sizes in popular models getting more play so they could easily be hidden from view inside a hook bait.

All members of the tuna family have sharp, keen vision with the ability to focus on objects near and far. In the offshore environment, waters tend to have good clarity although the total amount of available light decreases rapidly with increasing depth. The lens of the eye in deep swimming tunas can function in both focusing and light gathering and, with its nearly spherical lens, has the advantage of being able to nearsightedly examine objects up close while still having an ability for lateral farsighted acuity. Bluefin tuna, for example, are adapted for feeding in the depths as they have greater numbers of retinal light receptors than do other fishes. Added to this, they have blood vessels and contained blood at a temperature typically above that of the water they are swimming in. Hence, tissues like the retinal layer of the eyes and vision centers of the brain are continually warmed and function at a higher metabolic rate than do those of strictly cold blooded fishes. As a result, they have a much superior visual acuity, one you might

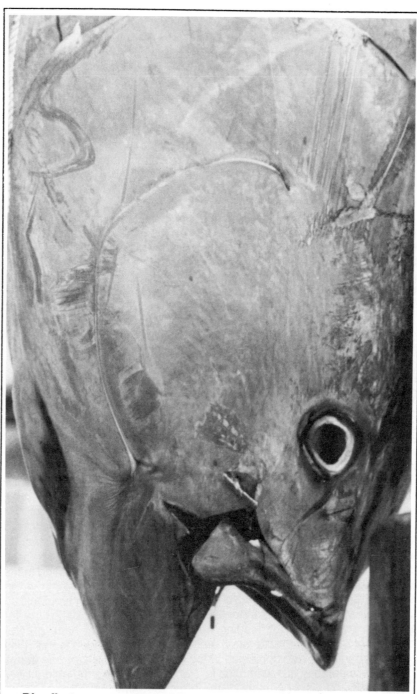

Bluefin tuna are adapted for feeding in the depths as they have greater numbers of retinal light receptors than other fishes.

not readily anticipate, which can cause them to shy away from a crudely presented lure or bait.

At anchor and chumming, with fish darting through the chum line, is a situation most tuna fishermen dream of time and again. When this finally happens and you don't get those anticipated bites, it's most probably a result of those tuna or bonito seeing the line, leader or hook, etc. It's for this reason anglers aboard the *Prowler* typically employ lighter monofilament lines than one might use ordinarily. The reason is action. Sure, we bust a lot of fish off, but we usually go home with a fish or two, which wouldn't have happened had we fished only the larger diameter lines. We use smaller diameter mono in green, clear, blue and pink, depending on water clarity, light intensity levels, feeding depth, etc.

Lines and leaders that have taken a few fish may no longer elicit strikes as a result of their becoming scratched (refraction) or frayed (opaque) or colored (bottom paint). This isn't much of a concern during hours of darkness but certainly is during daytime hours under bright light conditions, especially when fishing in the upper levels of the water column. If there's any doubt in your mind, strip, cut and retie.

For many years "mouse traps" helped to take those larger fish (bluefin) in the chum line with lighter lines, lines that would, if fished straight to the hook, quickly chafe and cut. The typical mouse trap allows one to employ a short section of heavy leader, typically light braided cable, at the terminal end. Folded up along the shank of the hook, this short section also would be hidden within the bait. After a strike, it's pulled out with the lighter monofilament now many inches away from their teeth. This is a very effective technique when it doesn't foul upon itself to bring many leader-shy fish to the transom.

Another tool or technique that has enjoyed some success is that of the "tuna bomb," a means whereby lighter lines are prevented from becoming chafed or cut. This apparatus is placed on the line and kept near the rod tip when fishing, in either one of several fashions, and is deployed following a strike. Basically, the weight of the bomb carries the anti-chafe tubing to the hook and protects the light line from those sharp teeth.

Looking up from the audience at the magician and his assistant, you could not readily see the suspending wires against the black backdrop curtain as they, too, were black in color. You could likewise mask objects in the water column by spraying them with a coating of flat black spray paint. Sinkers, tape, swivels, cable, wire, etc. suddenly became invisible, prompting those much desired strikes. A technique or trick, if you wish, painting hides any connection to the bait.

A number of years back an incident happened that cemented firmly into my mind just how well bluefin tuna can see. More importantly, how it affects whether they will bite or not. Anchored and chumming near a well-known highliner, my party and I watched as this particular crew constantly had either a bite or fish on. They were medium size fish, not really prompting an extended battle, particularly on 130 pound class tackle. Try as we might, we only had several bites with a single fish. With the glasses on every move they made, I watched a number of things new to me. A few days later, after considerable thought, several revelations came to mind, with nearly the

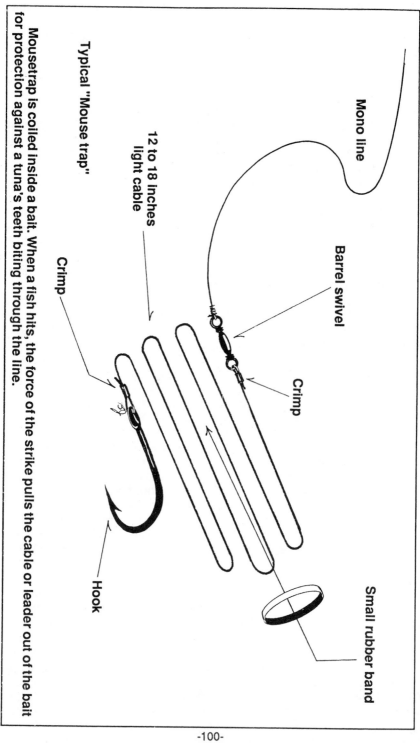

Mono line

Barrel swivel

Crimp

12 to 18 inches
light cable

Crimp

Typical "Mouse trap"

Hook

Small rubber band

Mousetrap is coiled inside a bait. When a fish hits, the force of the strike pulls the cable or leader out of the bait for protection against a tuna's teeth biting through the line.

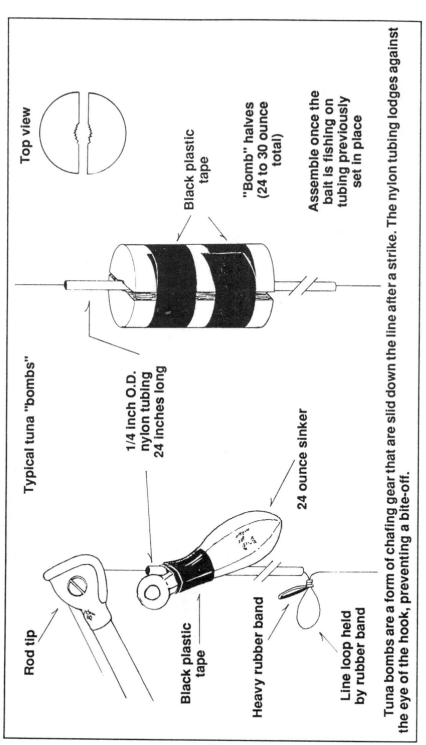

Top view

Typical tuna "bombs"

Black plastic tape

"Bomb" halves (24 to 30 ounce total)

Assemble once the bait is fishing on tubing previously set in place

1/4 inch O.D. nylon tubing 24 inches long

24 ounce sinker

Rod tip

Black plastic tape

Heavy rubber band

Line loop held by rubber band

Tuna bombs are a form of chafing gear that are slid down the line after a strike. The nylon tubing lodges against the eye of the hook, preventing a bite-off.

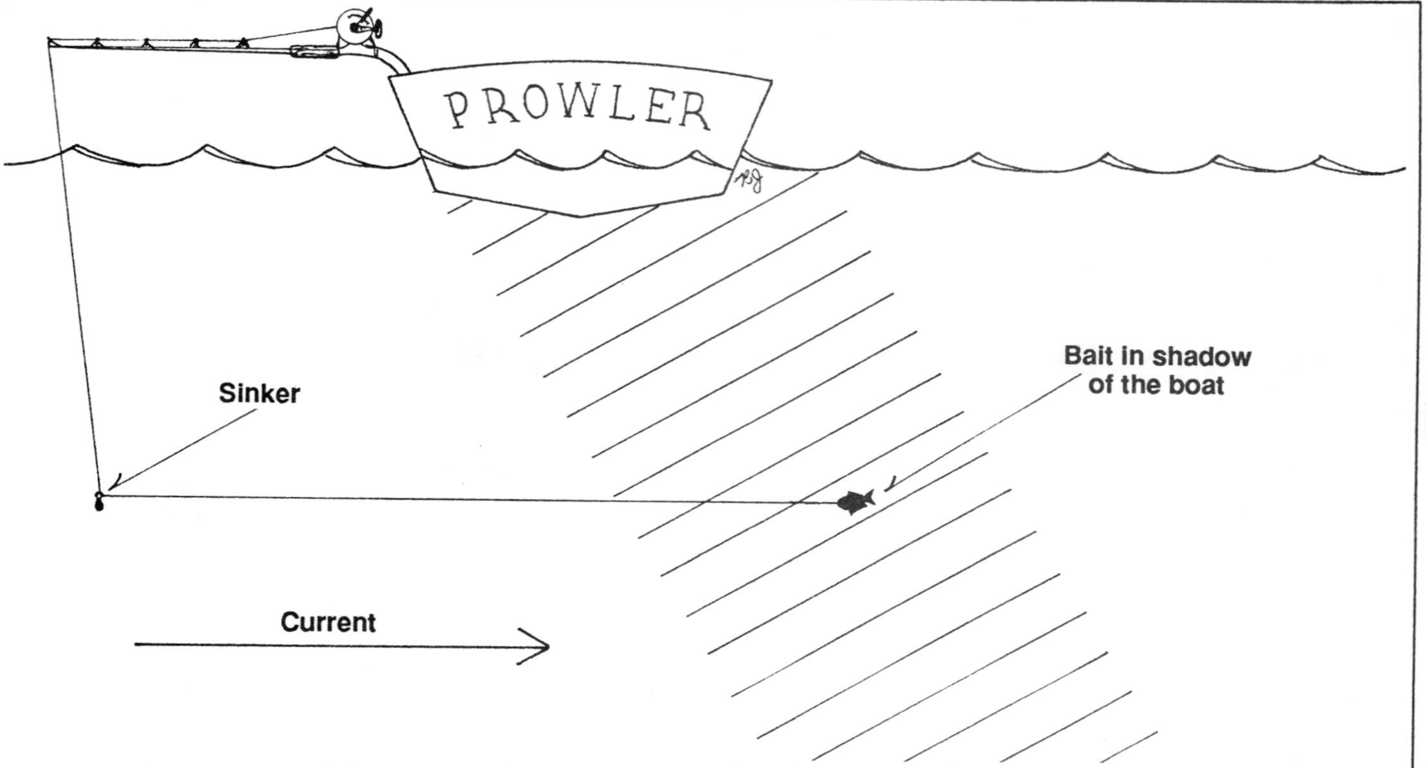

By placing a bait in the shadow of the boat you can hide the leader and hardware from the tuna's keen eyesight.

Sinker

Current

PROWLER

Bait in shadow
of the boat

same conditions again on the tuna grounds, only this day I had a competitor (charter boat) anchored nearby and it was our turn to give 'em a lesson, as they say. With high numbers of medium and near giant fish in the chum line, under bright conditions in the upper levels of the water column, these fish were very wary of the standard terminal tackle. Those fish could easily spot that heavy leader coming from the hook bait. Imagine now as these fish searched for a suitable meal, their swimming into and out of the shadows caused by those anchored boats above them. Imagine now the *Prowler*, measuring 35 feet by 12 feet, casting a nearly identical sized shadow beneath it as the sun climbed toward its summertime zenith. As those fish swam into and out of the shadows, their ability to see was clearly hampered. Remember that time you missed that pair of dark shoes on the closet floor because they blended in with the darkness? How about that time you simply lost sight of the ball in the early evening growing darkness on the ball field?

You can achieve the same results by placing the hook bait and the near portion of the leader in the shadow beneath the boat. Here the bait and attached leader become much more difficult to see, unlike that in the open with totally visible light filtering down. A bait set in this fashion is well downtide from the sinker weight with the near portion of the leader in dim light. A fish swimming up into the current perhaps sees the bait far enough away from the sinker so as not to shy away and the bites can come with relatively high frequency. As you might imagine, this entire situation is dependent on existing conditions, such as current and wind direction and velocity, light intensity, numbers of fish, swimming levels, etc.

In the wake of a boat trolling at high speed, disturbance of the ocean surface produces white water and these air bubbles produce light refraction and shadows. As a result, as seen below by members of the tuna/bonito clan, surface lures most probably become partially hidden and obscured. Subsurface lures with a covering background veil of refracted light and shadows make hooks and leaders more difficult to see. Up against the lighted surface fish see a silhouette, diving, darting, zagging, etc., that too obviously attracts and excites. I wonder how many times, in all the years high speed trolling the ocean surface, both tuna and bonito would rise to near surface levels and swim along and behind offerings. But, for whatever reasons, mostly attributable to their visual acuity, they lost interest and faded away into the depths without our ever knowing they were there.

Slow speed trolling for those larger tuna species does not afford us the luxury of hiding the somewhat heavier lines in a white water wake turbulence. What with bars and heavy mono or wire leaders dragging through the surface, offerings are many times visually perceived to be unnatural and shied away from. Line elevation reduces this behavior which has now suddenly become recognized by those who routinely author tuna articles for the glamour fishing magazines. Needless to say, it doesn't take much inventiveness to figure out a means of accomplishing such.

As described earlier, hook orientation in a slow trolled bait/lure can be critical, for reasons of unnatural silhouetting or surface seaweed collection. Both of these situations appear to reduce and/or eliminate potential strikes due to keen eyesight. For these reasons, careful attention is paid to this detail by those routinely successful while trolling.

Another situation, one commonly adjusted to by those routinely fishing stationary lines in the depths for tuna, is that of a line/leader choice. The concept here is that, as depths increase, visible light decreases, allowing for the use of a larger (heavier) diameter leader in the hopes that visual acuity in the depths becomes reduced. In other words, use 100 pound test mono leader at the 40 foot level, a 150 pound test mono leader at the 80 foot level, and a 250 pound test mono leader at the 120 foot level.

Bringing this chapter to a close, I must relate an episode that profiles human behavior, that of stubbornness and its affect on success. Have you ever come into an area of the fleet that is experiencing a bite in progress and, while the anchor line is coming tight, you begin to see several fish in your chum line or mark them under the boat? Anxious to get a bite, your first hook bait and its trailing leader is set out immediately. Let's say this bait is on 125 pound test mono as are the second and third baits, soon fishing. You continue to see or mark fish, yet you receive no bites. The boat nearby now has another fish on and still no bite. Marking fish at levels similar to your baits, you know they are in the strike zone. Giving in to your suspicions, you pull in that 125 pound test mono and replace it with a hook bait on 100 pound test. It may be awfully light line for good sized fish with a good chance of busting them off. Changing the other leaders still produces no strikes. Another nearby boat has its second fish on while you become increasingly frustrated, stubbornly refusing to believe that your baits are being ignored due to the line (leader) being seen. Finally, you pull in the bait and replace it with an 80 pound test mono leader. Even before the line fully straightens out in the current, you've got a fish on.

Many will argue that you've got to test the visibility of the leaders on any given day, starting with the heavier ones and working on down until you get the bite you're looking for. It's a common practice and a good one. But why did we wait so long to make changes when we suspected full well what was going on?

CHAPTER ELEVEN

Diamond Jigging

About halfway through my Tuna Behavior slide program, I profile those deep jigging techniques used for catching several species of tuna and bonito. Many in the audience know only of taking cod, pollock, halibut, etc. by this method from the cold waters of the Gulf of Maine and envision a stiff eight foot rod, Norwegian jig with teaser, and a pair of tired arms. They were surprised that this technique not only works for these speedy gamesters, but also at the relatively light tackle that is employed. They were further surprised to learn that sizeable tuna can be taken on relatively small jigs armed with small hooks.

All sizes of bluefin have been hooked while deep jigging and are probably the easiest to take by this method. Bluefin are followed closely by the common or green Atlantic bonito, then the false albacore. For whatever reasons, yellowfin tuna do not take a jig as readily as do others, but they can be caught in this fashion.

Having caught only a few bigeye, mostly in the trolling mode, has given me only little opportunity to try deep jigging. We routinely have no luck diamond jigging longfin albacore, even when around in good numbers. For whatever reasons we have little or no luck deep jigging for mushmouths or oceanic bonito even though we suspect they may be in the general area in fair numbers above the plankton layer of a thermocline.

The typical jig for tuna fishing is small and light. A good sized school bluefin may test the wire end loops and swivel so if there's any question as to construction quality it's best to replace with a sturdy brand. As a rough guide, two to three ounce jigs on 30 pound mono are fine for bonito. Four and six ounce jigs on 50 pound test are used for school bluefin and small yellowfin. Eight ounce lures on 100 pound test are favored for medium and larger bluefin.

The typical tuna jig has a free swinging hook rather than a fixed one. The hooks used are either a single Siwash, Mustad #9510XXXS or a treble Mustad Superior #5517. A 4/0 Siwash is about right for a four ounce jig and a 2/0 treble for the six ounce lure.

Hooks should be kept needle sharp with small, inexpensive Mill Bastard style files like those made by Nicholson. Files should be routinely sprayed with WD-40 prior to storage.

If fish are to be tagged and released, we use the single hook but, if they are destined to be steaked out, we use the treble which is much harder to get out of a fish.

With the first multiple bite of the morning, the throttle is finally brought back to idle in gear and both anglers are quickly instructed as to what to do while others wind in and retire their rods. With school bluefin suspected, jigging outfits are readied as these fish are brought closer to the transom. Peering down into the wake, the first of these school bluefins can be seen and is quickly taken, a fish of about 20 pounds. Soon, the second fish appears and,

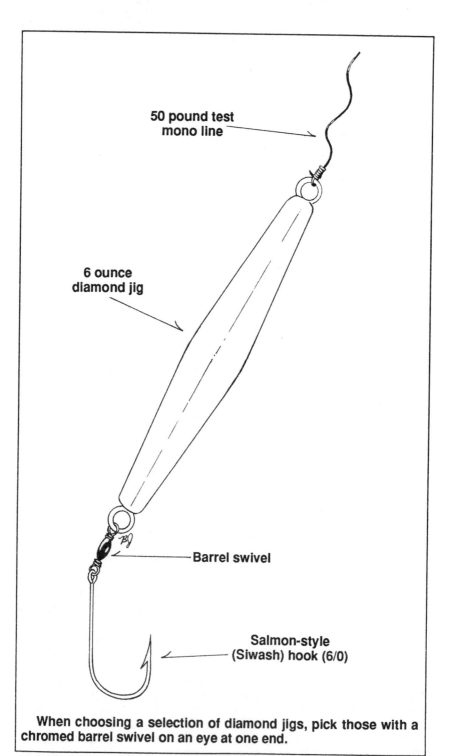

50 pound test
mono line

6 ounce
diamond jig

Barrel swivel

Salmon-style
(Siwash) hook (6/0)

When choosing a selection of diamond jigs, pick those with a chromed barrel swivel on an eye at one end.

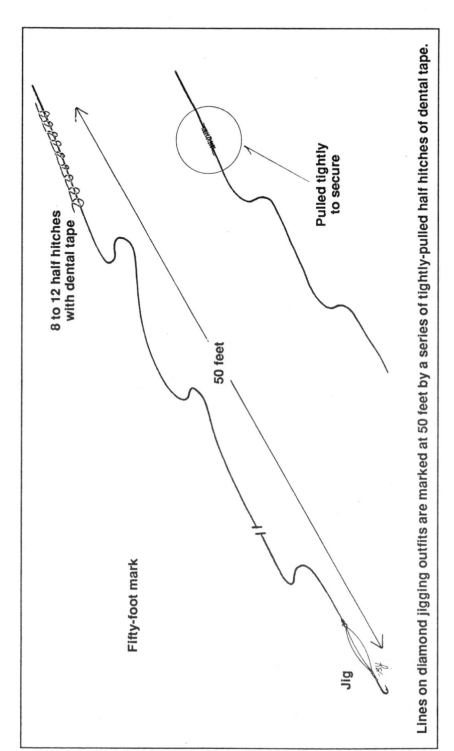

8 to 12 half hitches
with dental tape

Pulled tightly
to secure

50 feet

Fifty-foot mark

Jig

Lines on diamond jigging outfits are marked at 50 feet by a series of tightly-pulled half hitches of dental tape.

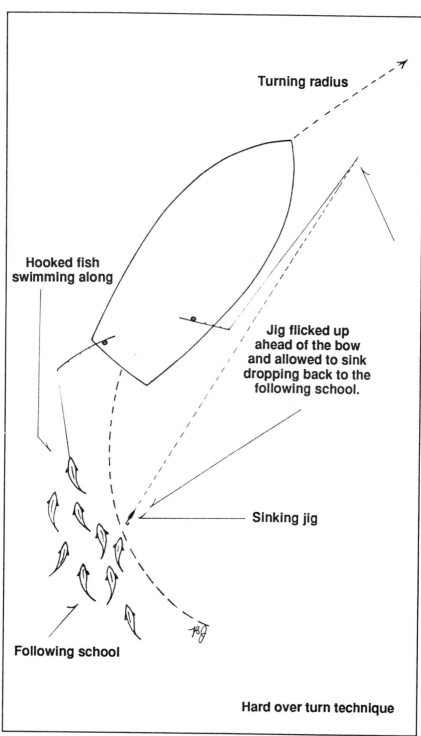

Turning radius

Hooked fish swimming along

Jig flicked up ahead of the bow and allowed to sink dropping back to the following school.

Sinking jig

Following school

Hard over turn technique

trailing behind and below, are good numbers of curious companions. With that, the crew is instructed to observe all actions carefully and the boat is put into a full, hard-over turn. Instructions are given to the angler to just keep his fish swimming along deep behind the boat, retrieving line only as necessary.

The first jig is cast up towards the bow, then allowed to settle. The lure is stopped at a prearranged "mark" on the line. Each mark on each jigging outfit consists of series of tightly pulled half hitches of either dental floss or dental tape approximately 50 feet from the jig. Over the years I've found the 50 foot level to be about right to jig fish following along after a hooked companion.

The tackle for jigging on that particular day was 50 pound line on a 6/0 Penn Special Senator. The mono was tied directly to the jig and cut back and retied after a day's fishing. Checking for frays and retieing is mandatory and don't forget to readjust the 50 foot mark after you've cut away six or so feet of bad line.

Fluttering down, the jig stops around the 50 foot level but is soon elevated to 40 feet by the slow forward motion of the boat. Jigged easily, a fish is seen to charge out of the school and grab the lure. The angler is guided to the corner of the transom and instructed to keep his fish on. If we lose this "lead" fish, the rest of the school will depart. The original hooked fish is now about spent so we land him and keep the other in the water, all the while readying a second jigging outfit. When the second lure gets to the payoff zone we get a hookup right away. When another fish comes to boatside, the tagging gear is readied. Sometimes you can keep this procedure going quite awhile.

Late summer can find the development of major ocean areas with a definitive plankton layer, usually in the lower levels of a thermocline, typically 35 to 40 feet below the surface. At times, members of the tuna and bonito family can gang up on those juvenile fish and squid that forage the plankton community. Frequently with slicks, storm petrels and shearwaters as biological indicators, the trolling and catching of these smaller fish can quickly become routine. Finding an area that looks good, perhaps with several trolling hookups nearby, and with little or no wind, you can do some drifting and jigging. Again, use a premeasured, marked line, adjusting depth to keep the diamond jig in and above the plankton layer. You want to make a forceful upward sweep of the rod tip a distance of four to six feet and then drop it quickly, allowing slack so the jig can flutter down, perhaps simulating an injured sandeel, tinker mackerel, etc. On a 12 or 20 pound outfit, smaller members of the tuna family can be fun. About the time you mention the absence of school bluefins, one usually jumps on, and on light tackle, offers a considerable challenge. Jigs with a trailing Limerick hook and tubing or those on a heavy mono or wire leader, a setup commonly used for bluefish, just does not enjoy much action from the bonito/tuna. My guess is the hardware is readily discerned and shied away from by these gamesters.

Probably the most common means of taking tuna diamond jigging is that while at anchor and chumming. In fact, it has saved the day, so to speak, on many occasions, not only with action but fish as well. Critical here is that the jigging take place at the depth fish are marking. It's a tiring effort, especially when done for extended periods and tests one's skill at time of hookup.

Anchor lines, too, can become wrapped and/or fouled, necessitating taking the outfit forward, usually happening when conditions start to roughen.

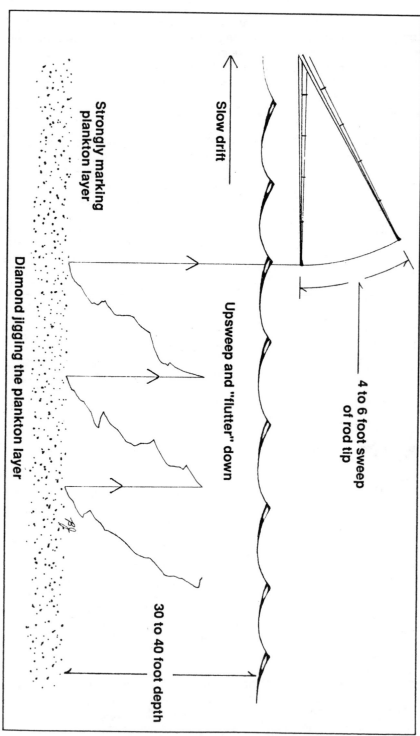

Slow drift

Strongly marking
plankton layer

Diamond jigging the plankton layer

Upsweep and "flutter" down

4 to 6 foot sweep
of rod tip

30 to 40 foot depth

Yup, you guessed it: a tricky place to be with the drag eased back so as to enable you to handle the outfit, turning it one way, then the other, trying to figure out in which direction it encircles the anchor rope. Trying to stay on the slippery, salt-laced foredeck attached to the fish can be quite a challenge with most anglers prudently returning to the cockpit for safety reasons, unless, of course, you're told to stay there because of another fish on back aft. Watching line grease off the reel, one might wonder if there will be enough water and reel drag on the line to turn this fish before coming to the end of the spool. One thing in your favor is that reels like a Penn International 30TW or 6/0 Special Senator allow for considerable capacity (425/525 yards of 50 pound test). If far removed from other boats, line drag due to water resistance can be an ally, but you'd better be prepared to spin that reel handle quickly when the fish doubles back at high speed.

The light weight of the jigging rod and reel with high line capacity are two key factors for success. Believe me, you simply cannot jig a Penn International 50W outfit for any length of time due to its weight. A rod sporting high quality, ungrooved ring guides and a roller tip, six-and-a-half feet long, 20 or 30 pound class, with a medium soft tip seems popular and more than adequate to do the job on fish under 100 pounds when in skilled hands. Again, a vigorous upward sweep is not absolutely necessary. It's more important that you drop the rod tip quickly so as to allow slack for your relatively small, lightweight jig to flutter down; a skill to be developed, for sure.

When choosing a selection of diamond jigs, pick those with a chromed barrel swivel on an eye at one end. It is to this swivel you attach your single or treble hook and use the other end for direct line attachment. The swivel, in my mind, accomplishes two things: it puts your line terminal end just that much further away from those sharp teeth, and, probably more important, allows for twisting and leveraging that would otherwise tear the hook out or open a ring eye or break a light copper wire jig eye.

A few years back, with massive sandeel populations, we enjoyed a long tuna and bonito season with bluefins predominating. Many fish were in the 80 to 130 pound range those first years and readily took our diamond jigs offered in the depths. However, we also had good numbers of giant bluefin in this bait as well. One particular day we found one attached to one of our eight ounce diamond jigs on 50 pound test straight to the lure. Oh-oh, what do we do now? A strong angler, still very early morning, a bow mounted chair in front of the center console and eager crew members were the answers. Bust 'em off or chase 'em was the question. Someone said something like "chase 'em, what the heck, we've got all day." This, of course, was before bluefin were worth any serious money. So, off we went, chasing after a fish that later, much later, tipped the scales at about 350 pounds. In fact, it was early evening by the time we got back to the marina with the fuel gauge needle no longer bouncing on empty, just stationary on the big red E. A thrill for the angler, for sure, but not quite the way to take a fish that size. Fortunately for us the tackle held together while we wore this fish down and gaffed it at boatside in a near-dead (fish and, nearly, angler) condition.

So, keep in mind that this technique of deep jigging can be employed in a variety of situations and offers another means for success.

Catching yellowfin tuna on stand up tackle requires a certain amount of ability.

CHAPTER TWELVE

Stand Up Tackle

Yellowfin tuna fishing (chumming) had been red hot the last few days and, anticipating another busy day, I was down to the boat a bit early to attend to a few morning details. Anticipating the arrival of my charter momentarily, I was looking dockward frequently during my work and spied the forward-most member of the group as he appeared. My first reaction was an "oh, dear," as he waddled along, an overweight and out of shape corporate type, brandishing a matched pair of stand up outfits. In my long career, I have become a fairly good judge of talent, even before they step aboard. Hearing a boisterous "we're going to get 'em today!" I mumbled a quick "God help us" under my breath and then welcomed this well-meaning neophyte aboard. Little did he know just how much talent was going to be required of him before this day's end.

For most of my career I have been a proponent of standing up to one's quarry, with the obvious exception of giant bluefin tuna fishing. This technique allows one a number of advantages, all of which will be addressed shortly. However, this requires the angler to possess some physical dexterity, balance, quickness, etc. which I simply call talent.

Against a 500 pound bluefin, most would opt for the big game chair, a footrest and the bucket harness. The drag pressure that has to be applied to equate the stamina of this species simply cannot be done by the average angler with stand up gear. In a fleet of boats, with myriad anchor lines, one has to apply drag pressure of 40 or 50 pounds or more in order to lead a fish along and out of the fleet. Once done, and without the threat of interference, the boots can be put to such a fish. A scorching run can then be handled without threat of loss of the fish to the ground tackle of other boats.

On the other hand, if you are focusing on fish that could weigh upwards of 200 to 250 pounds, stand up gear in the 50 pound class is more than adequate, assuming you have the advantage of a good captain and crew. If you're in an outboard powered boat, the one at the helm must answer to your directions promptly; if in an inboard boat, one without the encumbrances of trim tabs, and if a party boat, willing patrons to let you pass by in your efforts to follow your fish.

Catching a fish such as a yellowfin tuna on stand up tackle implies a certain amount of style, know-how, ability, etc., transcending that level of talent of the average offshore tuna angler. No doubt about it, accepting the physical challenge of bringing a fish boatside necessitates the appropriate tackle along with familiarity with and understanding of it. Well documented today, this west coast development of standing up to the fish came about as a result of their multiday pursuit of albacore and yellowfin by the faster party boats out of San Diego in southern California. With no big game chair to assist them, tackle and techniques evolved to the present state that allows for anglers to easily subdue present day record yellowfin. It can be safely

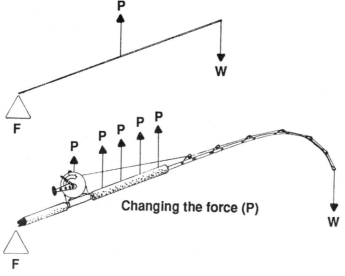

F = Fulcrum
P = Force (upward)
W = Weight or load (downward)

Typical third class lever

P

W

F

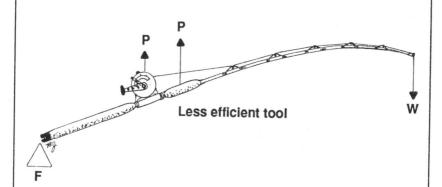

P P P P P

Changing the force (P)

W

F

P P

Less efficient tool

W

F

Mechanical advantage of stand up tackle versus conventional trolling gear.

stated that catching a tuna or billfish on stand up tackle in the 12 to 50 pound class affords one a sporting challenge. True, we hear and read about a few today brandishing 80 pound class stand up gear, but these individuals, in my opinion, are in the realm of overdoing it for publicity purposes. In my opinion, 30 and 50 pound class stand up tackle for the various tuna species easily tax the more accomplished anglers today.

Years ago, boats in the Pacific tuna fleet had crews that were fitted with waist belted leather thongs, bamboo poles with attached lines and jigs. Once in the midst of a school of tuna, they would scatter anchovies. As a result of the feeding frenzy, fish would take the offered barbless jigs, and then, by supreme effort, be lifted out of the water and back onto the deck of the boat. At times it required two crewmen with poles to a single jig because of the size of the yellowfin. Stand up tackle and techniques were in their infancy but many lessons were learned from the jackpolers. Today, rods are shorter and support star/lever drag reels. The leather thong has been replaced by gimballed belly/thigh pads and shoulder harnesses.

Just because the guy anchored up next to you and chumming for the smaller tuna has a set of 80 pound class rods out (overkill), stationary in a Rybo or Murray Chair, don't for one minute think he has an advantage over you in terms of tackle, unless, of course, the quarry exceeds a quarter ton. For the smaller tuna, stand up gear has several advantages and offers, as previously stated, greater angling challenge. Armed with probably the most popular harness equipment, Braid, you stand an equal or better chance of success, but only if you have clear freeway for your tackle and are competent with your equipment. As someone once said, "if you want to be good, you've first got to be good."

Proponents of stand up tackle recognize a number of requirements if they are to be routinely successful. One, they have to be prepared to move and follow the fish, whether it be in the cockpit of a pocket sportfisherman or on the deck of a party boat. Secondly, a shorter rod and its softer tip has a much shorter working length than the standard trolling outfit. As a result, you have less clearance for the line if you have to work around an outboard motor, trim tabs, chines, etc. No doubt about it, some physical agility is required if and when you come up against these obstacles. Leaning and bracing oneself against various parts of the boat have led many to wear knee pads, elbow pads, proper footwear, etc.

The typical stand up rod is a specialized piece of equipment, designed basically for battling fish while in the chumming or jigging mode. Unless fitted with an extension to the butt, many rods cannot be keyed into the standard gunnel mounted rod holder. Consequently, this style rod cannot be readily employed in the trolling scene. Use of this type rod then requires a belt which can be supplemented with a lower back or shoulder harness. This additional equipment can then allow the angler to apply additional drag pressure to the fish.

A few years back, when this tackle first made its appearance locally, I took a little time to test its effectiveness as to drag pressure. Armed with a Chatillion spring scale, I set out to see just how much drag pressure could be comfortably applied under ideal conditions. Lo and behold, it was considerably less than that advertised by one of the harness manufacturers,

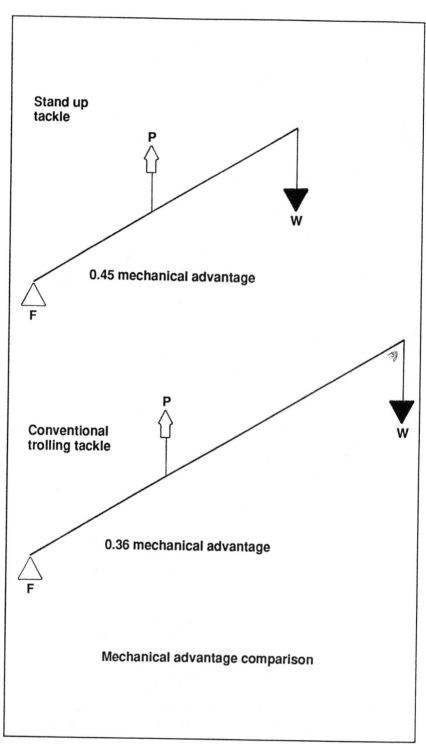

Stand up tackle

P

W

0.45 mechanical advantage

F

Conventional trolling tackle

P

W

0.36 mechanical advantage

F

Mechanical advantage comparison

although I'm confident their claim was genuine. For the practiced individual, 20 to 30 pounds of drag pressure posed no problem and did not interfere greatly with their ability to move around. However, as drag pressures climbed to 40 pounds and greater, one could not easily maneuver themselves and their tackle. But, when in a situation that forces one to move, drag pressure can be lowered for that period of time and then reapplied as the angler assumes his or her new position.

Let's take a quick look at the mechanics of a third class lever and compare your newly-acquired stand up rods to it. The rod butt nock in the gimbal of the harness becomes the fulcrum and the pull of the fish off the rod tip becomes the load or weight. Your hand on the foregrip along with the clipped straps from the shoulder harness to the reel becomes the force. Unlike a first or second class lever system, your rod can never have a mechanical advantage greater than one (1.0). However, it can gain speed with the weight (load) moving faster than the force. As an example, baseball bats and cranes fall into the same category as your fishing rod. All of the bones of the human body, with their attached tendons and muscles, also operate as third class levers but, unlike one of your bones, you can vary the spot in which the force is applied along the length of the foregrip. The standard trolling rod with its longer butt (12-1/2 inches) puts the center of the reel typically 16 inches from the butt end (nock) and this tends to reduce your mechanical advantage. With the foregrip extending just beyond the reel, the problem is compounded. The stand up rod, on the other hand, has a shorter butt and a much longer foregrip, allowing you to improve the mechanical advantage as compared to the typical trolling outfit. Last but not least, your stand up rod is shorter (five feet, six inches) than the standard trolling rod (six feet, six inches), giving you an added mechanical advantage in this regard as well. Some anglers focus on softer rod tips and variable ratio reels and longer reel handles for an even greater mechanical advantage should sights be set for larger fish.

Let's take a quick look at a setup I make available for my clients interested in tackling 100 pound yellowfin tuna on the chumming grounds. We use a Penn Tuna Stick measuring five feet, six inches, sporting roller guides and tip top. The rod is rated for 40 to 100 pound test line. On this rod is mounted a Penn International 30W reel holding approximately 400 yards of 60 pound test Berkley Big Game monofilament. For support we use either a Braid or Reliable belly harness and, should it be necessary, a Rip Off back harness with reel clips. Tuna, as well as sharks, have succumbed to this combination of stand up tackle and equipment, basically in the hands of novice fishermen, with some coaching.

Getting back to the opening scene of this chapter, I elected to fish three rods once the anchor hook took hold, one of which had to be hand-held due to the shortness of the butt. The individual who accompanied this tackle began to sound like a know-it-all and it took quite a bit of directed assistance before he got the nack of free lining a bait back in the slick. His inability was the result of his inexperience. Then it happened: a jarring strike that nearly wrenched the outfit from his grasp. Once the other outfits had been cleared, it appeared he had everything under control. Leaning back, he applied maximum pressure as this fish made another lengthy run and then reeled

Bonito fishing in the fall can offer fast action at uncrowded fishing areas.

furiously when it doubled back. With the mate shouting in one ear and the captain in the other, this poor soul simply could not do otherwise. With the fish straight down and circling, the first threat to its loss materialized but the gloved hand kept the line off the chine and quarter guards. Admonitions were made to keep the line off the chine by moving along the gunnel as the fish circled as the fish's behavior brought the line under the boat with each sweeping turn. With near maximum pressure, line was coming back onto the reel rapidly and we soon had color. Not too soon either for our angler was threatening to expire. Finally, a gloved hand assisted with bringing the fish close enough for the cockpit stick and, with that, our angler let out a war whoop as the fish was taken. The thought occurred to me that our success was due somewhat more to the sophistication of the tackle than to the talent of the angler but, together, it combined to make for a successful bite, thanks to the fish. In the hands of a competent angler, today's stand up tackle and equipment strongly tips the balance in his favor.

No doubt about it, stand up tackle is ideal for the small boat owner who has no room or desire to mount the smaller versions of a big game chair. Costing several thousands of dollars, or more, a chair and its footrest takes up a lot of room. Thus, money saved by avoiding expenditures for a chair can be used for a good combination of stand up tackle and equipment. This same tackle is ideal for that individual interested in making those overnight canyon runs on the growing number of party boats from various mid-Atlantic and southern New England ports. Although other tackle might do, it could put you at a disadvantage when you have to compete with others hooked up along that same rail. I think in this situation you would want the best equipment and tackle as you have the potential to fight and land a very sizeable tuna, possibly a valuable bigeye or yellowfin. Need I say more?

Author's tackle for diamond jigging bonito is a Penn Jigmaster with a five-and-a-half foot, light action, fast taper rod.

CHAPTER THIRTEEN

Bonito Bonus

Reaching into the five gallon bucket of previously cut butterfish pieces, I throw another handful overboard. While the anchor line is slowly coming tight, I carefully explain to the charter crew how to go about baiting and hooking their first Atlantic bonito of the day. With three lightweight conventional reel outfits at the ready, I explain how to pull line off the reel just a bit faster in free spool than the sinking rate of the bait in the current. If only a hint of a pickup, the reel should be engaged and thumb pressed onto the spool. I also explained that maybe by the third or fourth missed strike they'd become savvy enough to hang a fish.

Few who come into this fishery recognize the speed of these gamesters in the chum slick and, for that reason, blow or miss those first few strikes. Only after recognizing the necessary reaction speed does a wide grin finally cross their face as the clicker tells of line racing against the drag. No muscle needed here, instead, you want concentration and quickness. Perhaps in your area this year good concentrations of sandeels in 12 to 30 fathoms are attracting those fish we call Atlantic, common or green bonito *(Sarda sarda)*. Many of my clients over the years who hoped for battling a much larger fish were thrilled at the challenge of personally baiting, hooking and catching these smaller fish all by themselves on light tackle. After two or three decent fish in quick succession, the rod is then gladly passed off to another member of the party, for it's time to recoup from wrist and forearm fatigue.

On many days, being the first boat on the grounds gave us an advantage, that of drawing good numbers of fish into our chum line. Being in the right spot helped, like just on the edge of the bank in 15 or 20 fathoms. The visual acuity of this species simply has to be awesome, detecting that slowly settling column of cut bait from perhaps a dozen yards away, and perhaps more than one hundred yards away. Others nearby become visually aware of feeding and join in with the whole process snowballing. They come in waves with two or more fish on behind the transom at one time. We wait, minutes at a time, for another bite, quickly followed by another, and, perhaps, another. Fish move closer to the transom as a result of reduced competition (being caught).

Many days we had tons of fun with the party, opening a fish to discover a stomach nearly bursting with cut pieces of chum and accusing one member of the party of letting this fish eat us nearly out of all our bait. Or hooking another fish, with two or three hook baits (tails) in its gut and pointing to another member of the party, recalling all his missed strikes.

The tackle we use for bonito fishing is a Berkley Heavy Action Bionix five foot, six inch rod, Abu Garcia Ambassadeur 6000 reels and 12 pound test Berkley Trilene.

Throttling back, coming into an area just off the edge of a ledge (20 fathoms), we watch early morning birds working and lure, leader and line

Small pieces of butterfish are used for chum while tail sections are used for hook baits.

With the right conditions, flyrodders can experience some fast
bonito action.

quickly stream into the wake behind the boat. The lures are Hexheads in black and white and red and white and one ounce Sea Striker feathers in red and white. All six lines are then double checked as to distance astern and drag tension on the reels. The Furuno Chromoscope is watched for the first signs of fish and bait and, then, we hear shouts and directives as first one and then two more reels go off with chances possibly from a school bluefin. With the next bite, no doubt in anyone's mind that a much larger fish, then two more on, both of which are strong. At the transom, with angler peering into the wake, the first of two false albacore (little tunny) with directives to lift aboard, unhook and release. The second fish quickly followed suit. This last fish, first hooked, stays deep behind the boat.

"My guess is a school bluefin, maybe 25 pounds, probably a single (no trailing school) with others scattered throughout the bait this morning. Do you want to take it?"

With their reply, the fish is quickly gaffed, bled and slid into the well and lines stream astern once more as the washdown hose is used for cleanup.

No sooner had all lines started fishing than we had another bite, this time with five rods bent over, the crew frozen, not quite believing we had 'em on again. Short jokes, laughter, expletives, tangles, pulled hooks, etc and we were off to another super day of action with the smaller cousins. Like the tunas, bonito also come to the transom all lit up, as we say, displaying excitement in the form of transitory color markings and vertical bars. This coloration, however, quickly fades away upon their death. Scientists today believe these transient markings are a means of communication between those members of a school. As a result of their excellent visual acuity, in addition to detection of predators and prey, they also recognize these markings as they appear during feeding behavior, courtship and spawning. In the excitement of feeding, these fish, when lit up, convey the presence of food to others in the school, signalling aggressive feeding behavior. Scientists also are convinced that visual recognition of certain permanent body markings (stripes) may help a fish to distinguish its own kind, as opposed to others closely resembling it, at times of spawning. There is no doubt in my mind that the "pack attack" (multiple bite) phenomenon, demonstrated by the various bonito species, has a complex visual behavior basis.

For us here in southern New England, action with the various bonito species typically begins in mid to late August, reaching a peak in September and then fading away in early and mid-October due to falling water temperatures. Frequently, this time period sees a number of storms and, with them, the disappearance of yellowfin and albacore. But, the high bait concentrations continue to see predation by members of the bonito tribe and, as a result, offer an excellent opportunity for fast action.

Grabbing another hook bait, the file-sharpened point is carefully inserted into a tail section of a butterfish and rotated into place under the skin. Nearly hidden, except for the eye end, and carefully dropped overboard, it is allowed to settle away in the current. Pulling line just fast enough off the reel for slack, the angler concentrates on the line as it comes from the rod tip. Shaking the rod tip to facilitate movement of slack line from the reel through the rod guides, he watches for the first sign of the mono disappearing, a signal that a bait has been taken. With the reel enaged, he points the rod

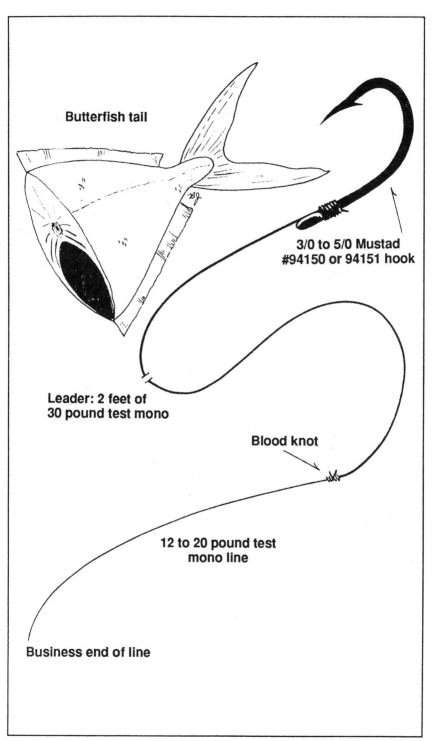

Butterfish tail

3/0 to 5/0 Mustad
#94150 or 94151 hook

Leader: 2 feet of
30 pound test mono

Blood knot

12 to 20 pound test
mono line

Business end of line

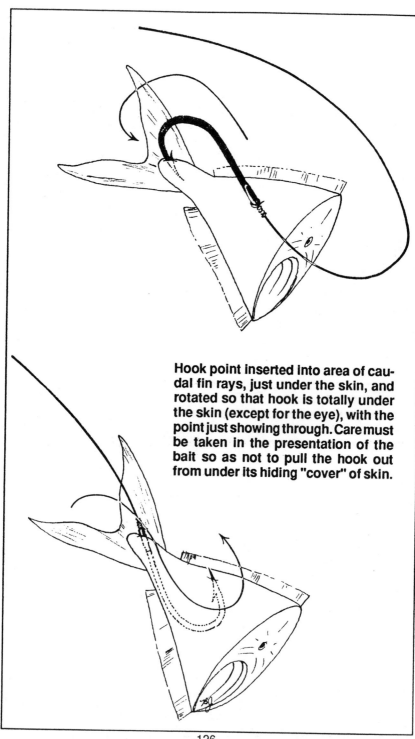

Hook point inserted into area of caudal fin rays, just under the skin, and rotated so that hook is totally under the skin (except for the eye), with the point just showing through. Care must be taken in the presentation of the bait so as not to pull the hook out from under its hiding "cover" of skin.

down the line and clamps his thumb on the spool, waiting for this fish to instantly hook itself. As the morning progresses, anglers become proficient at baiting and hooking a fish, we are on the lookout for fish flashing in the slick. With that, an ultralight spin outfit, six pound test mono and weighted streamer fly are readied. Instructions are to cast back into the chum line and give the lure (fly) time to sink, followed by an erratic retrieve right up to the transom. This technique of casting with ultralight tackle results in testing one's skill should and eight or ten pound Atlantic bonito jump on. Many times I've had to admonish an angler for cranking the reel handle while the fish spun the spool, taking line against the drag with the resulting nightmare twist to the line. However, for anyone to bait, hook, fight and boat any member of the tuna tribe, regardless of species and tackle, is quite an accomplishment. These smaller fish should not be disdained for they, too, require as much skill as that for their larger cousins.

Perhaps you, too, have witnessed this scene, that of several slicks on a near calm ocean with literally hundreds of birds working over them. Beneath the surface, racing through the bait and plankton, are skipjack tuna, little tunny, Atlantic bonito, school bluefin and bluefish. This area, alive with fish, is on the edge of a bank, ranging in depth from 90 to 120 feet, within a dozen miles from the beach. Trolling feathers and Hexheads had produced all of the aforementioned species and, for a change of pace, the decision was made to drift and jig with two to four ounce diamond jigs on light tackle. We use Penn 500 Jigmasters with 30 pound mono on custom five-and-half foot, light action, fast taper rods for considerable sport. And what adds to the day is sometimes, during a fall weekday, we have the grounds to ourselves.

Back on the grounds the next day, only this time my anglers are armed with fly rods. Fortunately for them there's no wind with a resulting calm sea surface. After profiling the previous day's action on our runout, I was stunned by the wealth of tackle displayed in my get ready admonition. Instead of a simple take-apart rod and single action reel, I witnessed nearly a dozen rods banded together in their cotton sleeves, with custom-made boxes of leaded reels, perhaps two dozen in number, each with a specific weight line and leader at the ready. Packets of flies, in various sizes and colors, told of many hours of preparation for this day. I watched in awe as rods, reels, lines, leaders and flies came together. I witnessed three anglers casting in different directions all at the same time from my cockpit, without any interference, and then listening to the sounds made by rushing line and backing as it sped through the guides upon another hook up. Soon I heard statements to the effect that these fish made all others look like slouches, bonefish included, and the question "why didn't we do this sooner?"

Arm weary by late morning, still with little or no wind, I got the directive to head in. I was more amazed at the talent, tackle and success of the crew than they at the willing resource available within their casting range.

In summary, if you are a small boat owner still looking for action after the departure of albacore or yellowfin from storm-cooled waters of early fall, consider chasing after the bonito. Typically these fish, which are excellent eating, can be found in bait rich waters in 15 to 30 fathoms.

ANGLER 6. Goldberg
FISH Big Eye Tuna
WEIGHT 248 lbs
BOAT Magnum II
CAPT. Rick Tshappy

Fishing the canyons for fish such as the 248 pound bigeye is one of the last frontiers for offshore fishermen. Photo courtesy of Gary Diamond.

CHAPTER FOURTEEN

Canyon Trip

In gear, idling along now, we could just make out the color of this last fish, head down and swimming along deep under the boat. The lever drag arm of the 80W Penn International reel was between the strike pin and full and the rod tip throbbed with the tail beat of this third and last bigeye that had ambushed our lures just prior to sundown in a little over 160 fathoms of water. Fishing an area called The Dip, located between Hudson and Block canyons, the *Prowler* was nearly 100 miles from home.

Fishing the canyons for yellowfin, bigeye, albacore, etc. is certainly one of the last remaining frontiers, if you will, for many offshore fishermen. Not all who venture offshore for tuna ever get a chance to fish the edge of the shelf for some of these once-in-a-lifetime fish. This particular chapter may give the reader some insight as to what goes on during an early summer trolling and early fall night chumming trip.

With the growing possibility the weather was going to allow for this first tentatively scheduled canyon trip of the season, a quick check was made of the extended forecast by the National Weather Service on both The Weather Channel and the VHF radio on Wx 1 and Wx 2. A report was being given for winds daily under 15 knots, with a large high pressure system building in and then becoming nearly stationary. As a result, fair weather with daytime winds offshore predicted as light to moderate but, more importantly, little or no chance for a low pressure system to sweep in bringing high winds and rough seas. The last place I want to be is offshore in the canyons in a nor'easter with its towering seas, cresting and running waves. The word uncomfortable simply doesn't describe it. As a general rule, winds up to 20 knots are fishable, but, after that, seas begin to build and enthusiasm quickly wanes, even in the larger and ultimate sportfishing boats of today. The widely-spaced isobars of the weather map indicated only little chance for even moderate wind and none for the chance of bad weather. With this, the next step was taken, that of making the necessary phone calls and pulling out the so-called check list.

Some of the items on this check list were normally carried aboard, some were added, and some removed. For example, that special box containing darts, gaffheads, tail ropes, block and tackle, safety lines, etc. was gone through to check all was in place. Additional items, such as a 151 quart Igloo cooler, diesel fuel containers, electrical and mechanical fuel transfer pumps, ice hold insulation (two inch Styrofoam sheets), take-apart shovel, handsaw, white canvas, tackle boxes with readied lures, extra bent butt outfits (total of seven), VCR and spare tape, etc. Food, fuel (additional) and crushed ice totalling nearly 1,000 pounds were some of the last items to come aboard. Items such as the twin trolling chairs that flanked the big game chair were removed and taken ashore, as was the working anchor, chain and line. No need to take this unnecessary equipment with its added weight to the edge. Finally, a careful check of the EPIRB and life raft to see all was in order as well as the latest copy of the satellite-generated sea surface temperature chart for the area.

Now underway, with all the gear aboard, attention should be turned to evaluating the latest sea surface temperature data, as well as making preliminary contact with those boats coming in from the edge of the shelf. One of the advantages we have over other areas is the large offshore fleet of commercial lobstering vessels. Many of these owner/operators are long-time friends and acquaintances who are more than willing to pass along valuable information. With morning reports from both private and commercial boats, it usually doesn't take too long to formulate a game plan based on their relayed information. With that, the numbers are punched in and the autopilot engaged. With a late morning start, we would be approaching the shelf slope by mid-afternoon. In just a few hours we'll listen to the updated weather forecast and be within radio range of those boats working and fishing along the edge. Reports from those private boats that trolled until midmorning before beginning their steam home this day are encouraging.

The typical game plan involves arriving on the shelf slope by mid- to late afternoon and then trolling that area we feel will be productive until well past the hour of darkness. At that time, following permission to tie up to a specific lobster trawl, we relax, have something to eat, catch a few hours sleep, all the while showing all lights (running, cockpit) and maintaining a watch. With the first hint of light in the eastern sky, lines are back in the water (unless we have a hot tip) and we resume trolling that area that was productive before darkness. Typically, this area changes overnight due to the current set, and, by midmorning with diminished action, we punch in the numbers for home. Back and cleaned up by early evening, the final entries are made into the log book.

On this particular trip, we had the seven bent butt 80W and 130 rods in place and fishing as we trolled through the lobster trawl gear late that afternoon. Several of the lobstermen we talked with indicated a sizeable longline fleet developing outside the northeast corner of Hudsons and, without any strikes, a decision was made to work out into deeper water with hopes of finding our first fish. Coming through some weed, the water temperature gauge jumped a couple of degrees. Back through that gradient, nothing; and then, returning, we had our first action of the day as two small yellowfin tuna attacked our lures on the port side. Quickly boated, they were bled and slid into the wet wells.

With no boats in our immediate area, all we had to go on was this thermal edge and the two yellowfin it produced. Back through the numbers the second time gave us another yellowfin and then, trolling eastward into steadily colder water, perhaps only a mile outside all the gear, we had a triple of bigeye tuna, which began this chapter. Trolling back toward the numbers of a specified trawl now in near darkness, produced one more fish, a small longfin albacore. Once tied to the gear, we began the job of heading and gutting the fish and getting them on ice. Once completed, we relaxed, and it wasn't long before the last of the ice cream and strawberries disappeared.

Well before the hint of first light, the aroma of coffee from the large thermos had everyone's attention and, under illumination from the cockpit

For a night trip to the canyon, our game plan usually calls for us to arrive on the shelf slope by late afternoon to find the appropriate lobster trawl gear to tie up to.

Canyon tie up as recommended by the Rhode Island Lobstermen's Association

Tie up line approximately 150 feet in length on the downwind highflyer following permission to do so.

Prevailing W-SW wind less than 25 knots. West end highflyer carries a flag, radar reflector and vessel name on the ball.

Commercial lobstermen (Point Judith, R.I.) are on VHF Channels 16 and 6 while working. They ask the tie up line (bowline) be in between the polyballs, not to the highflyer directly, on the downwind end of the trawl, i.e., east end of a trawl on a southwest wind. so as not to pull it up and across itself. Poly less than one-half inch diameter is suggested.

60 to 160 fathoms, from Hudson to Atlantis Canyons.

Trawls are set along the edge, not across it.

50 traps on a single trawl, over 1-1/2 nautical miles in length, or seven micro-seconds.

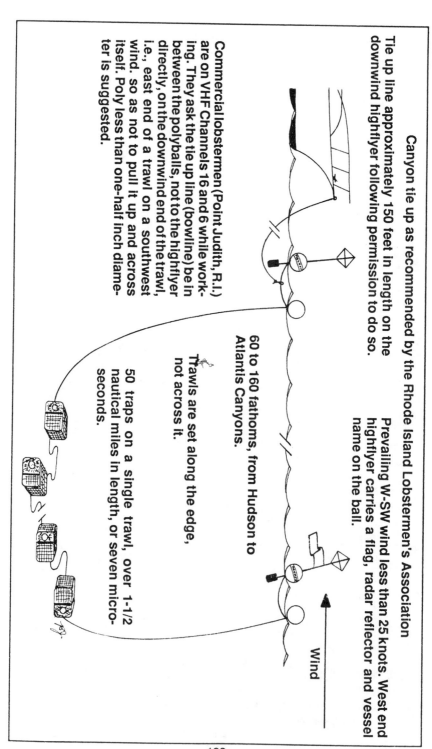

Wind

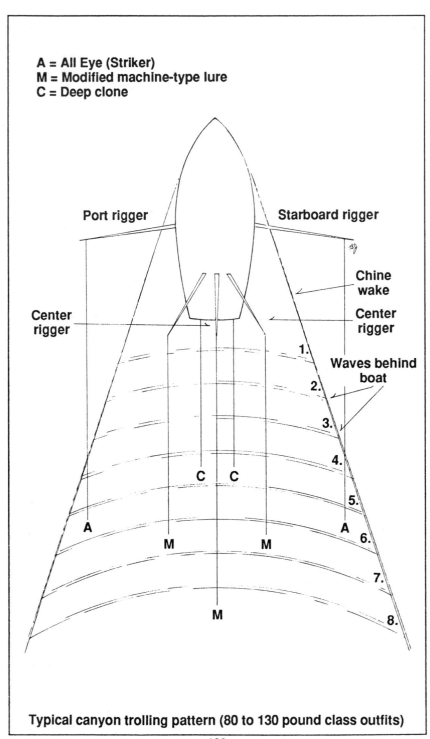

A = All Eye (Striker)
M = Modified machine-type lure
C = Deep clone

Port rigger   Starboard rigger

Chine wake

Center rigger   Center rigger

1.
Waves behind boat
2.
3.
4.
C C
5.
A   A 6.
M   M
7.
M   8.

Typical canyon trolling pattern (80 to 130 pound class outfits)

-133-

lights, the trolling gear was readied for going back overboard. A quiet evening with almost no wind allowed all a bit of rest and, as the radar showed the high flyer behind us, we resumed trolling. The typical pattern of lures that had worked before dark was again fishing with the approaching sunrise.

Those on-deck fuel containers with their extra fuel had been pumped into the main fuel tank while laying to on the trawl gear and were now stored out of the way below decks. Those valuable bigeye were iced in the insulated fish wells with the small yellowfin and albacore in the on-deck Igloo. To the east we heard our first morning report from a Montauk boat telling of no bites the evening before. With our report, they decided to head west in hopes of their first action.

It took several moments before anyone realized we had a fish on and, with that alert, the throttle was goosed and then pulled back, goosed, pulled back (surging) and, finally, brought back to idle in gear. A small longfin had decided to commit suicide on an All Eye fished out of a 130 pound class bent butt outfit off the starboard rigger. Back on the numbers of predarkness action showed only cold water (64°F) and, for reasons still not quite understood, the decision was made to troll back inshore to the northwest. Perhaps because of the evening current set and slightly warmer water while on the trawl gear, we began a troll back in that direction. Through the lobster trawl gear and into the tide rips as the depth quickly diminished to 70 fathoms. With this came our second, third and fourth fish of the morning, all longfin albacore. With that, the All Eye lures were exchanged for modified machine type lures and, once again, we had two more fish (albacore) on. Working that area until nearly 10:00 a.m. produced no more strikes and a decision was made to turn for home. In our eyes, a successful trip certainly, mainly due to those bigeyes below decks, but also for the ideal weather and resulting action.

In the fall, when water temperatures plummet due to an early northeaster or northwester, those fish inside of 30 or 40 fathoms move offshore into warmer water. By September here in southern New England, the edge of the shelf typically comes alive again with the various tuna species and, for whatever reasons, cooperate very well after dark hours in a chum slick. But I'm getting ahead of myself.

With the changing season, weather systems develop and move quicker eastward toward the Atlantic seaboard after Labor Day. With that comes a higher frequency of storms and those near inshore fish move off, again staging in the more suitable waters along the edge of the shelf. It's at this time, when offshore tuna fishing can reach a frenzied peak, one should be chumming after dark just outside of a major thermal gradient.

The typical game plan involves arriving on the shelf slope by late afternoon, searching out and finding the appropriate lobster trawl gear to hang on to. Frequently, good numbers of small dolphin congregate in the vicinity of the balls and high flyers and strike readily at light bucktail jigs spiced with a small squid strip. With approaching darkness, hook baits are readied and a chum line begun. Commonly the bite begins at dark and, if you're lucky, progresses through the evening and into the early morning hours. At first light fishing (catching) typically comes to an abrupt end and, with it, final cleanup chores, although a few boats may linger in preparation for a few hours of trolling. Back at the dock and cleaned up by early afternoon, the final entries are made into the log book.

Under the now strengthening illumination of the tower mounted deck lights, the 125 pound test mono off the 80W International on custom bent butt rods is fishing straight to the hook (Mustad #9174, 9/0) with selected large fresh butterfish for hook baits. Little did we know, fishing this particular evening, that the abundance of squid would create a near serious problem. These animals, likewise hungry, would attack and devour a choice hook bait in a matter of only a few minutes. As a result, our generous supply became exhausted in a few hours and we were forced to cull through the fresh frozen for suitable baits. As it worked out, it was only an annoyance as we had steady action through most of the evening right up until daylight.

Early on in the evening, we found ourselves inside of the majority of boats and chumming into a northwest current set. As the evening progressed, we experienced major changes in both the direction and strength of the current. Interestingly enough, those boats fishing right on the edge (95 to 100 fathoms) took a large number of albacore with only a few bigeye or yellowfin. However, those boats further up the slope (85 to 95 fathoms) saw fewer albacore with more bigeye and yellowfin hitting their baits. For those boats, their action on these fish occurred while the current was running northwest and then west. Once the current shifted into the southwest, only albacore were taken. As to why this happened I can only guess. That it did happen came as little or no surprise to those routinely doing this fishing.

During the course of the evening we made two major mistakes. The first was to tail rope and allow a mako shark of about 200 pounds to hang head down for a while from a stern cleat. The problem came with our attempts to keep our next fish (tuna) and the connecting line away from the chine with gloved hand. Yup, you guessed it. Even hanging nearly straight down, those mako teeth were still as sharp as ever. Judging from the struggle, it was probably another sizeable yellowfin similar to those already on the cockpit sole.

Our second mistake was to continue fishing with two fish already on, one in the chair and the other out of the gunnel rod holder. This third fish, obviously recognizing the confusion and limited number of people in the cockpit, immediately made for one of the other lines and, instead of three, we now had only one fish on.

Late summer and early fall water temperatures mandate that fish be bled and gutted almost immediately upon their capture if you desire high fish quality. As soon as possible after that, put them into a slush solution of ice and seawater to bring tissue temperatures down from their elevated levels created during the battle.

On the way home, we were hailed by the charter boat fleet for our overnight canyon report. We also passed the word along to our base station of successful fishing and gave an estimated time of arrival back at the dock. The last step was entries in the log book for another overnight canyon trip.

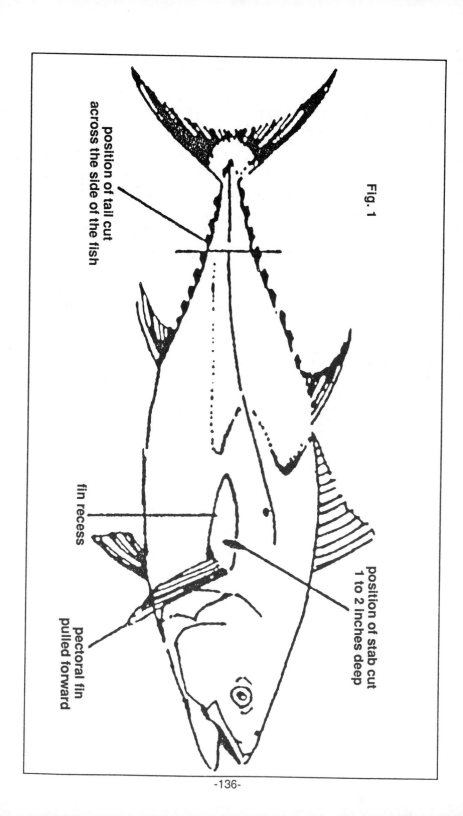

Fig. 1

position of tail cut across the side of the fish

fin recess

pectoral fin pulled forward

position of stab cut 1 to 2 inches deep

CHAPTER FIFTEEN

Handling Your Catch

*Courtesy of the Woods Hole Oceanographic Institution Sea Grant
Program, Woods Hole, MA 02543*

Acknowledgement. The Woods Hole Oceanographic Institution Sea
Grant Program supports research, education and advisory projects aimed
at promoting understanding and wise use of marine and coastal resources.
This information was prepared with funds from the NOAA National Sea
Grant College Program Office, Department of Commerce, under Grant No.
NA86-AA-D-SG090 to the Woods Hole Oceanographic Institution, WHOI
Sea Grant Project No. M/O-2 and A/S-8-PD. Fig. 1 was taken with permis-
sion of New York Sea Grant from "Tuna Handling Tips" by C. Smith and R.
Groh, 1983. Figs 2-11 were taken with permission of Hawaii Sea Grant from
"The Management of Yellowfin Tuna in the Handline Fishing Industry of
Hawaii: A Fish-Handling Handbook" by R. Nakamura, J. Akamine, D.
Coleman, and S. Takashima, 1987.

Introduction. Bluefin tuna are worth a lot of money if they are handled
properly. The value of this fishery is driven largely by the high demand for
top-quality, fresh tuna for the Japanese market. Fresh bluefin tuna is most
valuable when the fat content is high (generally between the end of July and
October) and when the fish has been handled properly to maintain its
freshness and appearance. You would probably be astonished to see how
particular the Japanese are about the freshness and quality of tuna for the
raw fish (sashimi and sushi) market. But if you have an opportunity to try
really fresh tuna sashimi (maguro), you'll soon realize why it's worth all the
fuss.

It may be difficult, if not impossible, for you to do all the handling
operations suggested below, because of your boat size, sea conditions, lack
of crew, etc. At least, try to keep mechanical damage of the fish to a
minimum, bleed it immediately, keep it cool and moist, and get it to a buyer
as soon as possible.

It's a good idea to check with tuna buyers in your area because their
preferred handling techniques may vary somewhat from those presented
here.

Important Points. The aim of much of the handling procedure is to cool
the fish quickly. Tuna keep their body temperature higher than the water
temperature, plus they heat up during the struggle when hooked. It can take
a long time to lower the internal temperature of a tuna, especially a large one.
The chances of tainting and spoilage (either "burnt tuna syndrome" or
histamine production, which can lead to scombroid poisoning) are reduced
if the body temperature is lowered as soon as possible. This is why rapid
removal of the blood and guts, which are warm, is important. In addition,
removal of the blood and guts reduces sources of chemical and microbial

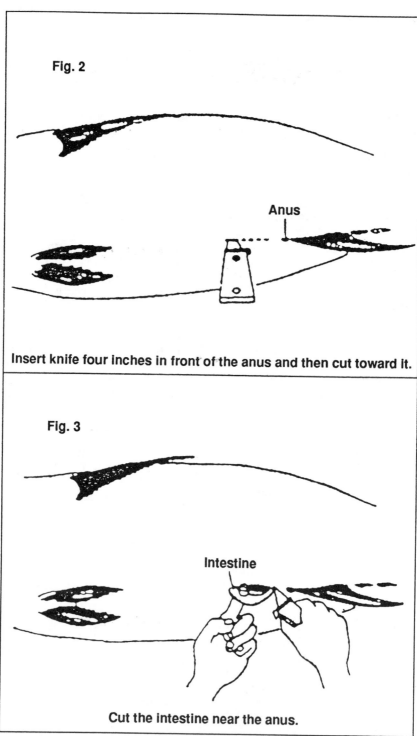

Fig. 2

Anus

Insert knife four inches in front of the anus and then cut toward it.

Fig. 3

Intestine

Cut the intestine near the anus.

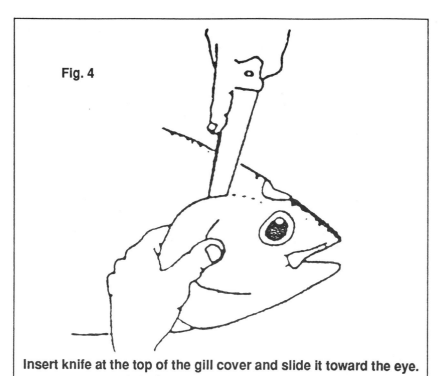

Fig. 4

Insert knife at the top of the gill cover and slide it toward the eye.

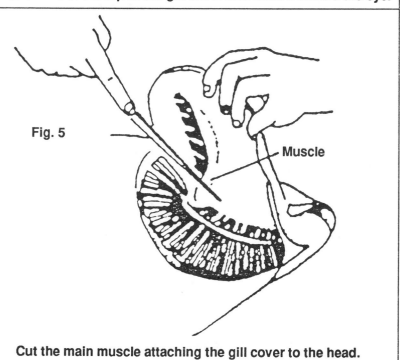

Fig. 5

Muscle

Cut the main muscle attaching the gill cover to the head.

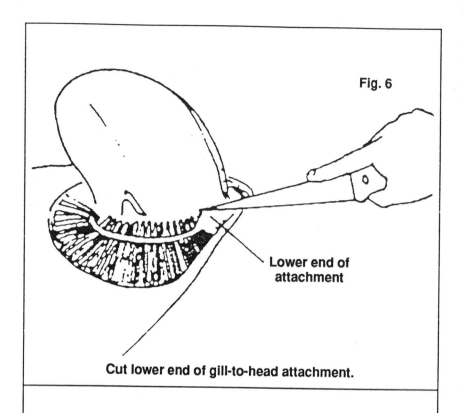

Fig. 6

Lower end of
attachment

Cut lower end of gill-to-head attachment.

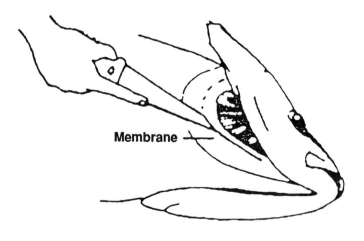

Fig. 7

Membrane

Cut through the membrane behind the gills.

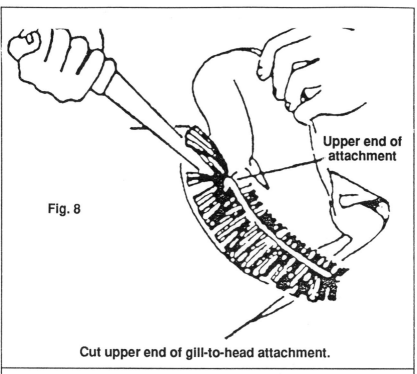

Fig. 8

Upper end of attachment

Cut upper end of gill-to-head attachment.

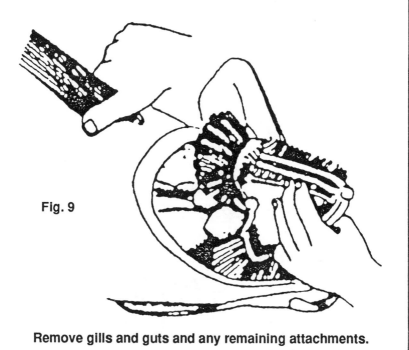

Fig. 9

Remove gills and guts and any remaining attachments.

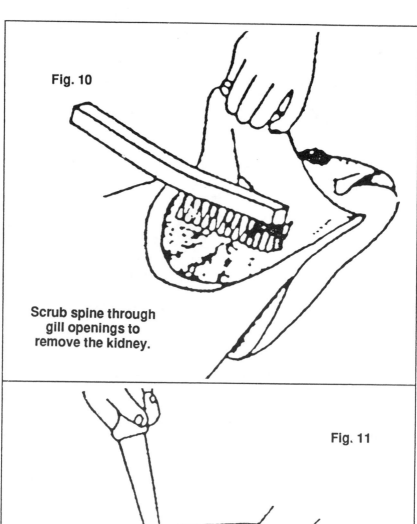

Fig. 10

Scrub spine through gill openings to remove the kidney.

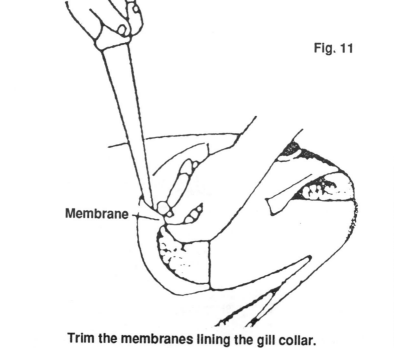

Fig. 11

Membrane

Trim the membranes lining the gill collar.

contamination of the fish flesh.

Do not move or touch the fish any more than necessary because the flesh bruises easily and will develop soft spots. Use of rubber gloves will avoid heat and oil from hands, which can discolor flesh. Use a clean knife. Keep fish wet and out of direct sun.

Tuna buyers are easily able to recognize when fish have been improperly handled.

Landing. For a giant bluefin tuna, this may be a tough job. Gaff the fish in the head region, through the lower jaw if possible. Hoist it aboard, trying not to bang fish on side rail. Treat side of fish that was pulled in over rail as the "bad side." Lay fish on its bad side on a smooth, padded (foam, blanket, rubber,etc.) deck surface away from hot deck plate and engine heat, being careful not to damage the fish on sharp objects or angles.

If fish is too large to be handled, hoist it by the tail and make bleeding cuts in tail (see below) and rake the gills. Tow it alongside the boat, head first if possible, in a way that will keep the fish from banging against the boat and so there is no "bow" in the fish which can cause tissue damage to the flesh. Get the fish to a buyer as soon as possible. Check your radio for tuna buyboats in the area.

Stunning. Immediately stun the fish with a hard blow (club, bat, mallet, rubber hammer, etc.) to the soft spot between the eyes. Obviously a large fish cannot be "babied" in this regard. Do your best, keeping your safety first. Immobilize the fish by deadening the brain and nerves. Push a sharp metal spike (ice pick, screwdriver) into the brain, which lies under the soft spot between the eyes, and twist it around to destroy nerve tissue.

Bleeding. Tuna should be bled as soon as possible to reduce internal temperature and to develop desirable color contrast of the flesh. Do not disturb the heart, as its beating will help pump blood out of the fish. Lift the pectoral fin and about one hand width behind its base make a vertical stab cut 1 to 2 inches long and 1 to 2 inches deep to cut the large artery in the mid-line of the fish *(Fig. 1)*. Make a shallow cut across each side of the fish in the tail region between the third and fourth dorsal finlets *(Fig. 1)*. Cuts should only be deep enough to sever the main artery located just under the skin in the mid-line of the fish. Keep the fish wet so the blood flows freely. Bleeding requires about five minutes.

Gutting and Gilling. Guts should be removed as quickly as possible, particularly from large tuna, to reduce internal temperature. Make a straight, four-inch long slit in the belly, cutting toward the anus, just deep enough to open the belly cavity *(Fig. 2)*. Do not cut through the anus so as to minimize exposure of flesh to digestive acids and bacteria. Reach into belly cavity and pull out the three "chords" (intestine plus two gonads) and cut them off near the anus, so contents do not spill in gut cavity *(Fig. 3)*.

Guts can sometimes be removed fairly easily at this stage if you have a deck hose with good water pressure. Place the hose in the belly slit. The water pressure will often force the guts out the fish's mouth. If so, cut the guts away. If this fails, the guts must be removed through the gill opening after removing the gills. The flow of water inside helps to cool the fish and minimizes staining of the valuable belly flesh from digestive juices.

Lift gill cover and make a cut at top of gill cover toward the eye *(Fig.4)*. Pull the cover back and cut the muscle attaching the gill cover to the head *(Fig. 5)*. Then cut lower end of the gill arch connections, but do not cut through the throat area as this will lead to distortion of the head area at rigor mortis *(Fig. 6)*. Cut around the gill membranes behind the gills up and down the length of the gill opening *(Fig. 7)*. Be sure to leave the crescent-shaped bone behind the gill area intact. Insert knife under gills, close to spine, and cut upper end of gill-to-head attachment *(Fig. 8)*. Perform same steps to remove gills from other side. Grab gills and remove them and the guts with a firm pull *(Fig. 9)*. Remove remaining guts, stripping membranes which attach gonads to body wall. Remove as much of the dark kidney along the backbone as possible. Scrub backbone with a stiff brush until white and flush with plenty of water to get rid of coagulating blood and slime *(Fig. 10)*. Remove the membrane surrounding the gill collar and remove all loose skin from gill exit *(Fig. 11)*. Gently clean slime from outside of fish.

The entire cleaning process takes about 15 minutes for an experienced person.

Chilling. If boat is equipped with a chill tank, submerge bled, gutted and gilled fish for one hour in an ice-seawater slurry made with two parts ice to one part seawater. Then remove fish and pack it with ice.

If you do not have a chill tank, pack body cavity with bags of ice immediately after cleaning. Cover fish with sheet of plastic and, if possible, completely ice fish over. Ice directly on the skin will cause blotching. If you do not have ice, keep the fish wet and out of the sun.

CHAPTER SIXTEEN

Marketing Versus Tagging

Nearly 30 minutes now since the strike, this fish shows little or no signs of tiring quickly. More amazing, with all the pressure being applied, the hook hasn't pulled, the leader hasn't broken, and the line is still intact. Where did this fish come from? Up until this point we had been experiencing bites from 65 to 80 pound yellowfin and were using 80 to 100 pound test mono straight to the hook. If this was a yellowfin, it was a monster and our chances of landing it seemed slim. But, should we succeed, the fish had the potential for considerable value.

Finally, this five year old fish is tail roped to a stern cleat and, along with congratulations, thoughts of what this fish might be worth dockside or on consignment in the overseas marketplace bounced around the boat. Later that day this fish tipped the scales (whole weight) at 189 pounds and we were to see other fish dockside well over 200 pounds taken by other boats in the fleet. Dressing out to nearly 150 pounds and paying, at that time, $4.00 a pound, the party later saw a check for nearly $300.

Should you focus on the sale of a tuna later in the day there are a number of things you must attend to for producing a quality fish. Follow the suggestions in Chapter 15. The outline material was provided by Sea Fresh USA, Inc. in Narragansett, R.I. It's typical of those distributed by tuna buyers in the mid-Atlantic and New England areas. The outline was prepared through the courtesy of the Woods Hole Oceanographic Institution Sea Grant Program. If the outline is followed carefully, it could go a long way to insuring top dollar from a tuna buyer. However, if targeting giant bluefin tuna, it might be a good idea to check with your potential buyer as to specifics of gutting and gilling. A fussy technician might not agree exactly with the outline tips.

Perhaps you've seen it, too, that angler or boat owner arguing with the fish buyer, arguing because the fish offered are of poor quality and worth little. Not fully realizing that the value of the fish lies with its size, body temperature, fat content, color, condition, numbers of other competing market fish, etc., an argument frequently winds up with the crew taking the fish to another nearby fish buyer, and hearing the same story all over again.

Those who go tuna fishing for profit quickly learn that monies paid are dependent on the fish going either into the domestic market or into the overseas (Japanese) market. The numbers of fish entering the marketplace, the time of year, etc. can strongly effect price. Just as with the small domestic market, large numbers of fish in the export market can quickly depress price due to supply. Probably more so than any other species, giant bluefin tuna have the potential to fluctuate considerably in value and it is for this reason buyers are more prone to ship a fish on consignment rather than risk paying

In 1988, the author received an award from the International Game Fish Association for his tuna tagging work. That year, Captain Anderson tagged and released more bluefin tuna than any angler in the world.

for it outright. When sold on consignment, the dealer earns a percentage of the deal with only minimum risk. You, in turn, see sale monies that reflect the price paid for the fish that day on the auction block. If only a few high quality fish come in that day, you stand to make out if yours is one of them.

During the 1989 season, for example, late season giant bluefin averaged $10 to $14 a pound for high quality (on consignment) in the overseas marketplace. However, on those days with little or no giant "maguro," a high quality bluefin went for as much as $40 a pound in the Tsukiji, Tokyo wholesale fish market.

However, the true value of our tuna resources does not simply lie in the marketplace. More so today one reads about the growing numbers of anglers focusing on these fish, whether from their own craft or from charter boats, and the monies generated in the pursuit of these animals. Tackle and equipment, boat sales, charter trips, fuel, bait, marina services, etc. have all been fueled by those wanting to tangle with these fish. Monies are spent, perhaps unduly, but with the thoughts that the sale of one or two good fish would offset some of these expenditures. Exactly how much revenue is generated annually by those in pursuit of tuna may never be known, but it must be considerable. In my opinion, and that of others as well, these fish are certainly worth more live than dead. With the realization of that fact, there's a changing opinion by many in the angling community. Today, if you waste the resource, you risk the potential for coming under considerable criticism.

Take, for example, that vessel and crew recently returned from an early summer canyon run. Scattered around the deck at dockside are a number of small and medium sized yellowfin tuna along with a nice bigeye pushing the 100 pound mark. All of these fish, you suddenly realize, are whole. Not one has seen a knife or saw, nor any ice for nearly 24 hours. They were simply taken without any thought to preparation and care. Now, as a result, they are worthless in the market or as table fare and the fish buyer walks away shaking his head. The disclosure came later that securing ice was just too much trouble and they had nothing to put it in anyway.

Take for example another boat and crew that has just returned from a late summer offshore trolling venture. The large coolers in this center console boat, along with the storage area under the casting platform, contain nearly two dozen small yellowfin tuna. With a continued bite of this sized fish now for nearly a week, the fish buyer no longer has a demand and simply indicates he doesn't want them. The market is flooded and the last wholesale price is down to 35 cents a pound. Handling and shipping fish at this price means a loss of money. Better to have tagged them and let them go than to kill them as they have been wasted. Released, they have the potential to age and mature and add to the total yellowfin population come spawning time.

This book, with its theme of how to catch 'em, doesn't mean abandonment of the conservation ethic. Just because you have a fish on the line doesn't mean you have to kill it. Now, don't get me wrong; if you have a sizeable yellowfin or bluefin, with considerable market value, by all means take it. But, if there's no market value, it makes no sense to kill it unless its for your own personal consumption. Tag it and let it go rather than wasting it.

Our boat has more than 20 years of effort on behalf of the National Marine

REGULATIONS AT PRESS TIME FOR LEGAL SIZES OF BLUEFIN TUNA

FORK LENGTH	ROUND WEIGHT	HEAD OFF LENGTH
Young School less than 26 inches	**Young School** less than 14 pounds	**Young School** less than 18 inches
School 26 inches but less than 57 inches	**School** 14 pounds but less than 135 pounds	**School** 18 inches but less than 40 inches
Medium 57 inches but less than 77 inches	**Medium** 135 pounds but less than 310 pounds	**Medium** 40 inches but less than 54 inches
Giant 77 inches or more	**Giant** 310 pound or more	**Giant** 54 inches or more

Fisheries Service's Cooperative Game Fish Tagging Program (CGFTP). Year after year we've tagged and released over 80 bluefin tuna per season. There were days we simply tagged and released all fish, even giants, because of the conservation ethic of that particular charter group. They had my full support for I knew my future business depends on healthy fish stocks.(Editor's note: In 1988 the IGFA presented Captain Anderson an award for tagging the most Atlantic bluefin tuna that year as well as tagging the most Atlantic bluefin tuna in the world for the CGFTP.)

Some years back, nearly 85 percent of those tagged fish recaptured annually had been previously caught by crew members aboard the *Prowler*. This is a good indication of the pressure on the bluefin fisheries, particularly with the advent of the growing export market for giant bluefin.

How do you get your hands on a few tags? Simple. Drop a line to Mr. Edwin L. Scott, NMFS, Southeast Fisheries Center, 75 Virginia Beach Drive, Miami, FL 33149 or call his office at (305) 361-5761. Mr. Scott is the director of the Cooperative Game Fish Tagging Program which primarily deals with the tagging of billfishes and tunas. You'll receive a packet of five tags, data cards, tagging needle, tag flag and a brochure explaining the history and purpose of this valuable program.

Each year the CGFTP publishes an annual report and the latest one (1988) indicates that program cooperators (anglers, commercial fishermen, etc.) and scientists tagged and released 549 tunas that year. Recent communication with Ed Scott indicates a significantly greater number of tunas were tagged in 1989, but we'll simply have to wait for that report to become available. Today, with a growing conservation ethic in the angling community, scientists are gathering more information than ever before on growth rates, population dynamics, migratory behavior. etc. as a result of this long-term program.

A few years back I remember talking with Ben Secrest of Aftco (known best, perhaps, for the manufacture of roller guides) at the New York Boat Show. The idea was to create a nationwide tagging tournament for a number of game fish species in which anglers would compete for prizes and awards while promoting conservation, research and sportsmanship. Now in its third year, this tournament utilizes CGFTP tags and, along with other species, recognizes the tagging of albacore, bluefin, yellowfin and bigeye tunas. Points are awarded for each fish tagged with prizes presented for participation and trophies to those anglers and captains who tag the highest numbers of a particular species. For more information, contact Mr. Ben Secrest, Aftco Mfg. Co., Inc., 17351 Murphy Ave., Irvine, CA 92714 or call (714) 660-8757 or FAX (714) 660-7067.

No doubt tagging as a conservation method is growing and anglers are becoming more aware of the various programs. In fact, the NMFS and the Virginia, New Jersey, New York, Maine and New Hampshire Sea Grant Marine Advisory Service, along with the Woods Hole Oceanographic Institute Sea Grant Program recently sponsored a tag and release workshop for the northeast region to inform those attending about issues, concerns, increased awareness, possible improvements, etc. Attending were angling leaders, club and association representatives, charter and partyboat operators, regional outdoor writers, fishery scientists, fishery managers, educators, conservation managers and anglers. As we move into the 1990s, I'm confident you'll see more events and programs explaining and promoting the tagging and release of tuna and other marine game fish species.

Let's take a quick look at those fishery regulations presently in effect for a number of Atlantic tuna fish species. At present, the NMFS is responsible for regulating and enforcing those laws adopted annually by Congress as recommended by the U.S. Secretary of Commerce following proposals by the International Commission for the Conservation of Atlantic Tuna (IC-CAT). For 1990, ICCAT established an overall quota for bluefin tuna in the western North Atlantic Ocean of 2,932 short tons. Of this, the U.S. portion is 1,529 short tons, with the authority to manage this fishery delegated to the Director of the Northeast Regional Office, Gloucester, Mass. Along with the bluefin, there are also regulations in effect pertaining to bigeye tuna and yellowfin tuna.

Should you plan to fish (rod and reel) for giant bluefin tuna, you must first obtain a valid Federal Fisheries permit in the general category for the vessel. Vessels permitted in this category start June 1 with a daily limit of one giant Atlantic bluefin tuna (ABT) per day per vessel. The season closes December 31 but, if the catch rate is slow, the daily catch rate could be raised to a maximum of three giants per day to maximize full use of the quota.

It is not necessary to have a Federal fisheries permit for your vessel if you have a school or medium bluefin in your possession. By both survey and fish buyer data compilation, those fish harvested are counted in the Angling Category quota. The season runs January 1 to December 31 or until the Angling Category quota is attained. The daily catch limit for this category is four school fish 14 to 135 pounds per angler per day, only one of which may be a medium Atlantic bluefin tuna. No more than four medium tuna may be taken by a vessel in one day even if there are more than four anglers aboard. The quota for this category for 1990 was 139 short tons (126 metric tons).

As for other tuna, it is illegal to remove the tail or fins of any size bigeye or yellowfin tuna prior to landing, although the head may be removed, and you may not be in possession of bigeye or yellowfin that weigh less than seven pounds rough weight unless otherwise authorized. No permit is required to fish for these two species at the present time.

Should you desire further information or complete copies of current regulations, write to National Marine Fisheries Service, Atlantic Tunas Program, Northeast Region, One Blackburn Place, Gloucester, MA 01930-2298 or call (508) 281-9344. Permit applications may be obtained by contacting the above address or calling (508) 281-9370. If you would like to be on the NMFS recreational fishermen mailing list, write care of Mr. Paul H. Jones at the above address.

Just as a reminder, it is illegal to have more than one giant Atlantic bluefin tuna in your possession for any reason unless declared so by written notice following that date. Also, it is illegal to sell any size Atlantic bluefin tuna to other than a licensed dealer.

Before concluding this chapter, a few words about the future of the tuna resources in the western North Atlantic. In my opinion, there's no doubt the bluefin tuna is in trouble, assuming the ICCAT Standing Committee Resource Statistics data is valid. By their own admission, ABT stocks are declining. Many believe that efforts presently underway in Congress to include all tunas under reauthorization of the Magnuson Act (MFCMA or 200 mile limit) will eventually reverse the decline of this species. As this is being written, the U.S. House of Representatives has passed an amendment to include tunas and we await the decision in the Senate. However, under the Atlantic Tunas Convention Act of 1975, the responsibility of conserving and managing tuna stocks is in the hands of ICCAT. With the exception of the bluefin tuna stocks, other tuna species are considered at this time to be healthy, without need for stringent regulations.

One of the first things I tell the students in my tuna fishing class is that only a few years back these fish had only little economic value and that traditionally they served as a recreational rod and reel fish. With the advent of the Japanese export market, rod and reel harvesting quickly gave way to other methods as their value increased. Bigeye and yellowfin quickly followed suit with monetary gain replacing the thrills and excitement as the reason for going tuna fishing. If we're not careful, these fish stocks too may plummet to all-time low levels as a result of their commercial value. For the time being, management seems to be working, however, the future is not altogether a bright one.

This final chapter offers 50 tips to make your next trip a successful one.

CHAPTER SEVENTEEN

Improving Your Success

The purpose of this final chapter is to summarize a number of concepts and offer suggestions for improving your success at catching tuna and bonito.

1. Far too many anglers fail to make frequent checks of the lures while trolling, not realizing that even way offshore a blade of eelgrass, even a tiny piece, on a hook results in no bites. A clump of Sargasso weed pulling and thrashing is obvious and readily attended to. Check the lures often and watch the water going by the sides of the boat for weed. The more seaweed you see the more frequent should be your inspections.

2. Unhooking a fish and tossing the lure and hook back overboard before checking it is a mistake. An improperly oriented hook will cause a lure to spin and be avoided by the fish. A hook bait with the hook pulled nearly out or point pulled through simply does not get many bites. A mackerel daisy chain with the terminal hook pulled inside the body has a poor chance of hooking a fish upon the strike. Take the time to routinely check the position and orientation of the hook.

3. Resist the urge to use an overly heavy line or leader. Remember, these fish have keen eyesight and will typically shy away from heavy gear. Experience dictates choice depending on fish size, light intensity, type of fishing, etc. Better to hook and fight a fish, with possible loss, than not to hook a fish at all.

4. Use the smallest hook you can get away with in the chumming mode; slightly larger for trolling and jigging is okay. A little effort in selection of the proper hook will pay dividends once you get the bite.

5. Frequently, when trolling a smaller feather or trimmed vinyl skirt (length) will prove to be more effective, particularly if the size of the lure approaches the size of the bait being fed upon.

6. Take the time to mark your lines and frequently check them as to length (50 foot intervals is good). Knowing how much line is out can help you evaluate your progress in the battle as well as assist time-wise without constantly measuring when in the jigging mode or on the chumming grounds. A felt marker or half hitched dental floss does the job as does a carefully tied blood knot (mono).

7. When slow trolling baits (squid, mackerel), keep in mind that the best boat speed is that which just keeps the chain or bar up and "working." Most boats, if twin engine, need to have one engine out of gear for this. If you own twin disc reverse gears, consider installing a troll valve. If you still troll too fast with one out of gear, you're faced with the in and out of gear routine.

8. When jigging for tuna, it's very important to allow the jig (diamond, butterfish) to fall away and flutter as it descends into the depths. This action excites and brings strikes from the fish, particularly as it descends through their swimming levels.These fish see best at the level at which they are swimming. If the fish are marking at 50 feet, that's where the jig should be.

9. Use the freshest hook bait available whenever possible. The same goes for cut chum bait. Sure, you've heard stories about catching fish on ancient bait but, for whatever reasons, perhaps eye appeal as well as odor/smell, the strikes seem to come quicker with the fresh stuff. Don't hesitate to freeze three or four hook baits per ziplock bag if you come across an abundance of high quality bait to be used that one day when nothing is available at the dock.

10. Should a fish take your line (mono) under the boat or along the chine, it may not fray badly enough to require immediate replacement but will carry some color with it from the bottom paint. As a result fish will shy away from it, so cut and retie if you can or replace, substitute, etc.

11. Take the time after boating a large fish to carefully inspect the leader (mono). It may feel alright but, in the battle, it has rubbed on the fish's body, across the gill plate, etc., leaving those line marks on the fish. More importantly, it has become scratched and no longer has the translucent qualities it started with. Simply replace the leader, if you use one, with a fresh one.

12. On those days when the bonito are zipping through the chum slick and you're set up for larger fish, put out a smaller bait on lighter line and see what happens. If high speed trolling and you suspect bluefin may be around, put a smaller lure or two out in the wake close behind the transom (third wave).

13. There are several excellent quality outrigger clips presently available but if you fail to check them for tightness or fouling you run the risk of missing the bite or, worse, damaging the outrigger. Spend that extra moment to test and inspect each one prior to their employment.

14. It doesn't happen very often, but when it does it usually results in a disaster. That's the use of an inferior quality hook (not forged) for sizeable fish. Be fanatical when it comes to style and manufactured quality of this item of tackle.

15. You should have at least one or several small files aboard for putting that extra sharp point on those hooks to be used that day. As they come out of the box is simply not the best and are usually in need of touching up. Use that same file on your gaff and dart points, too.

16. For more reasons than you can imagine, it pays to check the drag settings for tension and smoothness before, during and after the day's fishing. A grabby drag needs to be serviced before it gets the opportunity to lose a fish, not after.

17. Anyone with half a brain takes the time to fashion and use (by attaching at both ends) safety lines to their larger, more expensive, bent butt outfits. Most rod holders today are not designed to withstand 40, 50 or 60 pounds of strike drag in giant tuna fishing or high speed trolling in the canyon for bigeye. You wouldn't want to lose a 130 or 80 pound outfit overboard, now would you?

18. When it comes to slow trolling the bars and chains for bluefin and yellowfin, most inexperienced anglers fail to use a heavy enough strike drag needed to take the belly out of the line but, more importantly, to tear the rigged hook out of the bait and into the jaw tissue of the fish.

19. Many think that a slow trolled bait with its hook need not be concealed from the fish. Take the time to orient the hook so that it offers the least outline

to the fish below and behind the bait.

20. Some of the successful tuna fishermen spend a few winter hours spray painting (flat black) a number of sinkers, in different sizes, prior to wrapping in paper (for protection) for later use. A quick touch up, if needed, on the way out and they are ready to be used in the darkened depths for controlling line and bait depth.

21. If you anticipate tangling with an oversize tuna, take the time to test your tackle and gear by pulling real hard on it before putting it in the water. This will confirm the integrity of hooks, knots, snells, swivels, etc. Better to spend the extra time in preparation than bemoaning the loss of a super fish.

22. Way too often we hear of a good fish on and the line buries itself into the reel spool and we all know that usually results in the line breaking with loss of the fish. So, next time you wind on new line, make sure you pack it tightly under pressure back and forth on the reel spool.

23. Next time, while chumming, remind everyone, including yourself, to concentrate visually on the stationary lines and rods. If there is only a hint (rod tip bounces) of a strike, immediately turn the reel handle to take up any possible slack which then frequently results in the fish hooking itself. Otherwise, you may have what we call a "spit out."

24. Keep in mind that, along with eye appeal, a hook bait washes out odor/smell after a period of time. If available, replace any hook bait that you suspect may be washed out, particularly one with several hours of use.

25. With bent butt outfits in gear and fishing in their holders, give yourself a bit more of an advantage at the time of a strike by moving all the reel handles into a prior upward position so that they are easily grabbed. Adhesive tape on the plastic handle grips can reduce their slipperiness when not wearing cotton gloves.

26. Too many anglers fail to advise the person running the boat as to the whereabouts of the fish near the end of the battle. Keep the boat moving ahead slowly at leadering time so as to keep it out from under the boat, so as not to jeopardize fish loss to propeller or rudder.

27. In the trolling mode, frequently check the lines and lures to see that they are not fouled with weed, the hook(s) proper orientation, etc. so as not to spin and twist the line. Check also while chumming, particularly when fishing your line straight to the hook without a swivel.

28. When high speed trolling brings a strike or two or more, the memory button of the loran should be punched to record your exact position. Returning to that area where you had the bites is now easier.

29. Carefully watch your hook bait as it settles away in the chum line. If it sinks at a faster rate than the cut pieces (due to the added weight of the hook), either reduce the size of the hook or stuff a piece of Styrofoam into the hook bait, out of sight of course. A minute or two spent adjusting the sinking rate could bring immediate success.

30. For those of you who enjoy using braided dacron, take the time to set up a few "headers" (usually 300 to 500 feet in length) with double line already spliced in, marks on, and reversed on a plastic spool so that the tail end is ready to go should you fray or break or discolor a "header." A quick splice and you're back in business again.

31. You've been rushing all day; to get to the spot, to get the lines out. etc.

Now, with a fish on, don't rush to get it to the boat. More than any other reason, fish are lost at boatside for the lack of patience. So what if the fish takes line again? You'll get it back. Take that extra moment or two to let your tackle tire the fish. It'll be easier to leader and gaff with less chance of a breakoff.

32. Plan on doing some trolling with natural baits? Take the time to secure some Formalin solution or, better yet, salt to toughen up those baits. Several hours in the solution will do the trick and reduces the time necessary for rigging which takes away from the fun.

33. While trolling for either school bluefin or bonito, a short sweeping motion of the rod tip will increase the number of strikes when compared to a straight running, non-pulsing lure. The jolt of the strike with rod in hand more than makes up for the effort involved.

34. School bluefin tend to follow one another around so, with one of these close to the transom, look down in the water column to see if there are any school mates behind. If so, put that diamond jig outfit into play, keeping that one fish swimming along.

35. A good supply of leader or line should be aboard for chumming. As light intensity changes, so should the diameter of the mono and/or its color. If the depth at which your hook bait is fishing changes, so should the leader. With less light in the depths, the heavier the leader can be. Conversely, you should consider lightening the leader as you fish closer to the surface.

36. Take the extra time to set up a quick release mechanism when on the hook chumming for fish. You never know when, for whatever reasons, you'll have to respond quickly to the antics of an overly large, and probably valuable, fish.

37. Whether steaming along, looking for a spot to drop the anchor or high speed trolling, make it a point to look for fish as well as run the fish finder. This visual information can help you make a smarter decision about where to fish that day.

38. I've lost count of the number of times a few choice live baits out in the slick made all the difference in the world. A little extra time spent in the morning securing them is all it took. Take the time now to figure out how you can get a live bait to the grounds in your boat for next year.

39. Make it a rule among the crew that they treat all bites as tuna bites. More than once we came close to not reacting fast enough, believing it to be from a bluefish, shark, etc. And make sure everyone in the cockpit has their assigned duties when the strike comes.

40. Another rule is to alert others on the boat if there is any suspicion of a strike or bite. At times, diamond jigging, it's only a bump, but this results in a quick double check of tackle and gear which can make all the difference. Alert others so they can help judge if it really was a boil behind the port rigger chain, etc.

41. The last thing you want to do when high speed trolling for albacore, yellowfin, etc. is slow the boat down after a strike. Keep it going. In fact, surge it as this may bring that pack attack, resulting in two, three or more fish on.

42. Too many anglers and crews make the mistake of winding in the line once the boat is slowed to allow fighting a fish. Sure, if there's a tangle, but otherwise keep 'em in the water. It takes less time to resume fishing and, yes,

bites have come on lures subsurface just idling along during the struggle.

43. Once you've found a strong thermal edge, don't leave it. Chances are there will be a few fish nearby. If you see a prominent tide rip, work along its length. Check for signs of life, i.e., weed, birds, bait, etc. Thermal edges work much like fences with animals moving back and forth among them.

44. Whether trolling, chumming or diamond jigging, take a little extra time to verify all the gear is at hand and ready. It may be too late to go and look for that tail rope with the only fish of the day thrashing behind the transom or the bag of tags now that all these smaller fish have been located.

45. Make it a point to record conditions, loran numbers, water temperatures, fish, etc. in a log book. It will serve as a useful reminder if you note a needed repair, a new technique or trick, effective style of lure, etc. as well as remind you of mistakes to avoid in the future.

46. Avoid that common mistake of not bleeding a fish the moment it's attached to or is in the boat whether for personal consumption or for sale. Cover the fish from the heat of the sun or, better yet, get them on ice.

47. If you plan on tagging and releasing a few fish, have all the necessary equipment at the ready. Take the time to jab the tag into the proper area (back) of the fish. A tag in the wrong spot (belly) will most probably injure or kill the fish. Tow the fish slowly along chineside until the right moment comes.

48. A couple of overly large tackle boxes, perhaps one for trolling gear and another for chumming gear, will help keep things organized and facilitate transport to and from the boat.

49. Those plastic-coated wire ties make the job of coiling and storing those rigs a lot simpler and can end much of the confusion when being retrieved.

50. Be sure to give all tackle exposed to salt spray a good freshwater rinse at day's end. A quick wipe with a chamois and a spritz of WD-40 will help reduce the onset of corrosion and prolong the life of your favorite tackle and gear.

Acknowledgements

Special thanks to the following for their assistance in this effort: Len Belcaro, Richard W. Brill, Darryl J. Christensen, Albert Conti, Jim Fox, E. K. Harry, Bill Krueger, Bill Rauft and Norbert Stamps, Jr.

Indebtedness also to Capt. Dennis Sabo of Massachusetts Maritime Academy for giving me the opportunity to conduct a number of slide shows for their Tuna Seminars; to George Hawkins of the Rhode Island Marine Trades Boat Show and the New England Sportfishing Boat Show; to Tim Coleman of The New England Fisherman Fishing Shows; and many others who allowed me the opportunity to develop the slide/lecture program that led to this book.

Last, but not least, thanks also to my wife, Daryl Anne, whose patience, help and encouragement allowed me to bring this idea to completion.

About the Author

A Rhode Island resident since 1963, Captain Anderson lives in Narragansett with his wife, Daryl Anne, and owns and operates the charter sportfishing boat *Prowler* out of Snug Harbor Marina in Wakefield, R.I.

At present, he is the Director of the New England Offshore Sportfishing Tournament (NEOST), hosted annually by Ram Point Marina in Wakefield. He is a past president of the Rhode Island Marine Sportfishing Alliance (RIMSA) and has been a strong representative for business interests serving the saltwater fishermen. He is currently the Sportfishing Chairman for the Rhode Island Marine Trades Association (RIMTA) and was recently elected to the International Committee of the International Game Fish Association (IGFA) as their Rhode Island representative.

Concerned with conservation and management of marine fishery resources, he is presently advisor to the National Marine Fisheries Service (NMFS), Recreational Fisheries Committee for New England (Oceanic Pelagics) and was recognized recently for his outstanding tagging efforts of bluefin tuna for the Cooperative Game Fish Tagging Program (CGFTP).

A former high school teacher, he holds a Master of Science Degree in Fisheries Biology and is busy in the offseason authoring articles for such publications as *The Fisherman*. He is also the author of "The Atlantic Bluefin Tuna ... Yesterday, Today & Tomorrow."